On Her Soapbox

Also by Chonda Pierce

It's Always Darkest Before the Fun Comes Up

It's Always Darkest Before the Fun Comes Up audio

Chonda Pierce on Her Soapbox audio

CHONDA PIERCE

On Her Soapbox

ZondervanPublishingHouse
Grand Rapids, Michigan

A Division of HarperCollinsPublishers

Chonda Pierce on Her Soapbox
Copyright © 1999 by Chonda Pierce

Requests for information should be addressed to:

ZondervanPublishingHouse
Grand Rapids, Michigan 49530

Library of Congress Cataloging-in-Publication Data

Pierce, Chonda.
    Chonda Pierce on her soapbox / Chonda Pierce.
      p. cm.
    ISBN 0-310-22579-5 (pbk.)
    1. Christian life Anecdotes. 2. Pierce, Chonda. I. Title.
    BV4517.P415 1999   99-39362
    242—dc21   CIP

Published in association with Wolgemuth and Associates, Inc., 330 Franklin Road #135A-106, Brentwood, TN 37027.

Interior design by Nancy Wilson

Printed in the United States of America

99 00 01 02 03 04 05 /❖ DC/ 10 9 8 7 6 5 4 3 2

This book is dedicated to all preachers' kids everywhere
who struggle with getting on their soapboxes and
voicing to God how they really feel.
Go ahead, my friend. Let 'er rip!
The church will survive, and
God is longing to hear from you—the real you!

Contents

ACKNOWLEDGMENTS

I'd like to say thanks to those who make me what I am. These thank-yous may appear, at first, to be the same ones I gave out in my last book, but believe me, they are fresh, new, and well deserved. (It's just that you guys keep doing your jobs so well!) So thanks to Mike, Jan, Doris, Michelle, Cricket, Ruthann, Mike H., and, of course, the road mangler, Charley.

I'd like to use up most of this page to thank the people behind the scenes, those who have encouraged—well, more like "prodded"—me into speaking out, to even consider getting on my soapbox to begin with. They include:

The lady who told me when I was five years old that I wasn't very p-r-e-t-t-y, to which I promptly replied, "No, but I am real s-m-a-r-t." She helped me to understand early on that I can say what I think and God won't fall off his throne.

My first-grade teacher, who embarrassed me by calling me up in front of the class on the first day, bending me over her knee, and spanking me for my birthday. (And it wasn't even my birthday!) Because I survived that humiliating moment, I realized that my being embarrassed in front of thousands of people doesn't embarrass God for one minute.

Buddy Long, the long-haired surfer from Myrtle Beach on whom I had a crush when I was in the seventh grade, for never giving me the time of day. He helped me see that there are other fish in the ocean—and the one fish God had in mind for me was the best catch of all.

The man with no auto insurance who crashed into my first new car (I was nineteen) and creamed it only two hours after I had driven it off the lot. God used that fellow to teach me that stuff never lasts—maybe not even for two hours.

The men at the audition table at Opryland (a musical theme park in Nashville), who told me to "come back next year when you're not so skinny."

The woman who called to write a magazine article about me and who believed—and told me—that I was too old to do much in the Christian music industry. (God and I just laughed and laughed and laughed!)

The lady who called my office not long ago to complain that I had waltzed with my mother at the end of a show. That woman prompted my desire to hop up on my soapbox and to talk to God about all this junk.

You're all wonderful in your own special ways, and each of you has taught me some great life-lessons—whether you meant to or not!

Most important, I'd like to thank God. You're the best listener!

THE BOX
WITH A VIEW

I've never cared for heights. Even those scenic overlooks on curvy mountain roads make me woozy. And the only time the top of my refrigerator ever gets cleaned is when I forget I'm running bath water upstairs, and the tub overflows. But there is one place, way up high, that I don't mind going. When I'm there things look a lot different—clearer, I think—and that's up on my soapbox.

Oh, yeah, I have a big, old soapbox. In my mind it's bright yellow and orange and makes my blue eyes look even bluer. And it's funny how the thing works. The box is big and bulky, but it's easy to drag around, and the older I get, the easier it is to climb up on it to say a few words—words about my husband, David; my children, Chera and Zachary; or my mom. Then sometimes (since I'm already there) I might even have something to say about men who seem to have no time or energy to really repair something, but who are geniuses when it comes to rigging up an old broken washer or toaster so it continues to limp along, or about grandmothers who would punch out a biker if it meant getting in on the early shipment of the newest Beanie Babies. I get a pretty good look at stuff like that from up there.

When I was just a kid, my mom used to wear her hair up real high. "Big hair," we called it. She once told us the taller her hair, the closer to God she felt. If that's the case, then the soapbox in my mind is tall also, really tall (almost as tall as Mom's hair was back then). Since I'm already up so high, why shouldn't I go ahead and share these thoughts with God? He's interested, you know, in the small, the mundane, the trivial. Every story I share with God constitutes a moment in which I *talk* to God. (Funny how that works, huh?)

And when that happens, I can count on something taking place that's much bigger than any old soapbox I could carry around (something that makes my eyes bluer than they are). From up there, I can see things from angles I'd never seen before. Sometimes I learn things about others that I never knew; other times I learn things about myself. But one thing is always certain: I'm going to have fun. So move in close, listen up, and prepare to chortle and giggle, maybe even snort a time or two. (Grab a bookmark in case you need to take a break.) Because I'm up on my soapbox now, and I have a pretty good view. I can't wait to tell you how things look from up here.

COUNTING
FAT GRAMS

The only thing worse than being on a diet is being around someone who is on a diet. I get up on my soapbox whenever I think about it.

Now, I don't want to seem insensitive. After all, my high school nickname was Tweetie Bird, partly because of my high-pitched, squeaky voice and partly because of my skinny, knobby-kneed legs. So I know insensitivity when I hear it.

I never used to have to worry about my weight, but Mother says I have to think about diets now. Something about corn chips and being *almost* forty, but I don't know.

Anyway, what I'm talking about here is the career dieter. My mother has tried everything from Weight Watcher's to Slim Fast, from Dial-a-Meal to Melt-a-Meal—complete with some contraption that melts your food down to pill form. Don't ask. It's another one of those late-night Ronco deals for three easy payments of just $14.95 each.

Mike Smith has been my manager for about three years. He's an average-sized man over fifty—well over fifty. Most of our years together, he's been on a diet of some sort. Amazingly, he's lost nearly 113 pounds, but he's gained 112. On this roller coaster ride, he's eaten and not eaten all sorts of things. He tried the popcorn-only diet. No matter how good that stuff smells when you first pop it, the thought of popcorn for breakfast makes me ill. The cup-a-day diet. That one wasn't so bad because you could eat anything you could fit into a cup. Once I watched Mike cram a double-cheeseburger and large order of fries into a coffee mug.

The weekend David and I planned to go off to a cabin on the river with Mike and his wife, Jan, was the same weekend Mike began his no-fat-grams diet, or at least no more than twenty per day. On the five-hour drive Mike rode along, sipping his bottled water without complaints. He swirled the clear liquid in the bottle and said with a satisfied grin, "Not a single fat gram!"

"Good for you, Mike. I'm proud of you," I said, and I really meant it.

The cabin was in central Kentucky at the end of a long, dirt road—no telephone, no TV—but a fine fishing river about four hundred yards away at the end of a grassy field.

"This is great," David said, as he unloaded two big grocery sacks of snacks and burgers.

"Yeah," Mike chimed in, "we'll burn off some fat grams walking down to the river."

"Maybe we'll catch some fish, too," David said.

"You know, a two-pound catfish has only four fat grams," Mike said.

"Really? I didn't know that," David said. Mike was teaching us all.

Rather than walk, David and Mike *drove* the van to the river while Jan and I started supper: hamburgers and potato chips. The men came back without any catfish, so we threw a couple of extra burgers on the grill.

"I'll just have a salad," Mike told me, as I flipped the red meat over to brown.

"Are you sure?" I asked.

Mike frowned and nodded. "Yeah, I think it's best. Just one burger has eighty grams of fat. You add mayonnaise, and that's another twelve. What kind of bread is that, wheat? No? Then tack on another six."

David walked up, fanning away the smoke from the burgers. His cheek poked out like a squirrel's. That's how he ate sunflower seeds. "Hey, Mike, want some seeds?"

Mike's face clouded with fear. "Oh, my goodness, let me see that." He snatched the open pack of seeds from David. After studying the package, Mike announced, "Twenty-six fat grams per pack! My goodness, why don't you just go ahead and put a gun to your head?!"

"It's just sunflower seeds, Mike," David said and spit an empty shell off the porch. "We'll play badminton later and burn it all off."

Mike continued to stare in shock at David's fat-gram-filled cheeks. Then, shaking his head, Mike walked away, visibly upset.

That evening we played rummy. All was quiet when suddenly Mike announced, "You know, one Pecan Shortbread cookie has almost five grams of fat."

David whistled sharply.

I looked around the table. No Pecan Shortbread cookies in sight.

Without looking away from his cards, Mike announced, "Even a Fig Newton—full of fruit, mind you—has almost two per cookie." He discarded and concentrated on his hand as he regrouped his cards.

Jan seemed to ignore him, playing sixes and nines and discarding out. She took a bite from her bag of Cheese Doodles to celebrate. The snack was still in the bag, so Mike turned the package to read the label. "Wow, would you look at this!" He held the bag with one hand and stabbed at the numbers with his other. "Nine grams per serving, seven servings in a bag. That's sixty-three grams of fat in this one bag!"

"Okay, whose deal?" I said, and for a brief moment we all tried to forget about fat grams.

Later that night, I discovered that out in the middle of nowhere, in the woods, in Kentucky, it can get pretty dark and pretty scary. Noises are out there that either are drowned out in the city by other sounds or occur only out in the woods in the middle of nowhere.

It was late, very late, and everyone had gone to bed. And was it ever dark. I awoke for some reason; I thought I'd heard something. David was breathing, but that wasn't it. A scratching sound was coming from the kitchen, the kind of sound a mouse makes while gnawing through plastic. I held my breath and tried to remember where all the furniture was. If I had to jump out of bed, I certainly didn't want to crash into a rocking chair.

Scratch, scratch.

"David, did you hear that?" I whispered.

He didn't budge.

Scratch, scratch.

I gripped the covers and pulled them up tightly to my chin.

Finally, Mike's voice scared away my fear of rodents. "Can you believe this?" he said, his voice coming from the kitchen. "Just one Nutty Buddy bar has sixteen grams of fat. Oh, and look at these barbecue chips. One serving has—"

Then Jan, no longer quiet, no longer understanding, went off like a fire alarm—a fat-gram alarm. "LISTEN HERE, FAT-GRAM BOY, IF I HEAR ONE MORE WORD ABOUT FAT GRAMS, YOU'RE WALKING HOME.

HOW MANY FAT GRAMS DO YOU THINK YOU'LL BURN OFF THEN?!"

David sat up. In the dark I imagined his eyes bugging out, his mouth forming a little *O*.

For a long time there was only silence, no more scratching. After a while, the chirping of the crickets returned, and David eased his head back to his pillow. But before I fell asleep, I thought about what I had heard and wondered if, after that, Mike would even dare to *dream* about fat grams.

The next morning, I fried some eggs, and Jan laid some strips of fresh bacon in the skillet. Mike had brought along a cantaloupe for himself. No one said anything about what had happened the night before.

Finally breaking the eerie silence, Mike announced, "Give me two eggs and some of that bacon."

All eyes turned to him.

"Do you know how many fat grams are in that meal?" David asked.

"Yep!" Mike answered. "But I'm not doing that anymore." He dragged two greasy strips of fat from the stack to his plate. And we ate like pigs. When he finished, Mike pushed back from the table and dabbed his mouth with a napkin.

David was preparing himself a biscuit and some grape jelly when Mike cut a disbelieving glance his way. He whistled sharply. "Do you know how many *calories* are in that?"

We all ignored him.

"Do you know that you can gain two calories by licking a little, bitty postage stamp?"

Fortunately for all of us, this story ends well: Mike went on to lose lots of weight (I think he did it by counting carbohydrates), Jan got a new pressure cooker (that was during the phase in which Mike was laying off fried foods), and I got a chapter for my book.

We can count fat grams, we can count calories, or we can count peanut butter and jelly sandwiches. There's nothing wrong with counting, and I'm all for being healthy, but I don't want to be silly about it.

Now, I know Mike isn't the only one who has ever been concerned about his appearance—even I am sometimes. So when I get to feeling blue about the outside of me and seriously consider counting something (like bites of chocolate), I think about God's view of me. "For you created my inmost being; you knit me together in my mother's womb. I praise you because I am fearfully and wonderfully made; your works are wonderful, I know that full well. My frame was not hidden from you when I was made in the secret place" (Psalm 139:13–15).

I love knowing that I am "fearfully and wonderfully made." We *all* are—even you, Mike. So why not tell the Lord about your fat grams and the calories on a postage stamp? The rest of us are sick of hearing about it!

Anyway, that's how things look from up here on the soapbox.

I've Never Met a
Beanie Baby I Didn't Like

All I needed was a jar of pickles—one pickle, actually, but I set out to buy a whole jar. I needed them for egg salad, David's second all-time favorite food. He was a bit giddy when I told him about my plans. So early that morning I made a trip to our neighborhood store for pickles.

Have I told you that shopping isn't always my favorite thing to do? Oh, some days that's *all* I want to do, but other days I can't stand it—like the day before Christmas, the day after Christmas, and double-coupon day at Kroger's. Those are the days that separate the saints from the sinners. But don't get me started on that—I'll get on my soapbox about checkout mania in another chapter. For now let me share something else that's on my heart.

Our neighborhood store sells more than just food. It goes in for things like lawn chairs, fishing worms, and Beanie Babies—yes, Beanie Babies. Ever since our super-duper Wal-Mart started to sell eggs and bologna right alongside hunting supplies and electronics, I have a hard time going to the store to buy "just a loaf of bread." After I return home with my bounty, David will stand in the kitchen moaning, "You spent $25.32 getting one loaf of bread?"

I learned on this particular morning that every Thursday a shipment of the newest Beanie Babies comes in. Apparently, this is a big deal. (Pickles probably come in only once a year, and no one ever pays attention.) I pulled into the parking lot, and if it hadn't been for David's teary-eyed, I-don't-deserve-you-for-a-wife smile when I had told him about the egg salad, I'd have turned right around and gone back another day. Because people—mobs of people—were lined up at the doors, waiting for them to open.

A big-boned, strong-looking woman was at the front of the line. Her hair was still in curlers. She had dark circles under her eyes, as if she hadn't slept much lately. Under one arm she held a pillow. Behind her the long line of people ran down the length of the sidewalk, along the storefront, and then out into the parking lot, weaving through and between cars—old people, young people, big-boned and skinny, men and women, teenagers and seniors. The line ended at the little rack where people park their buggies when they are finished with them.

Farther down the line from the big-boned woman was a pair of older ladies, sisters probably, gray-haired and wearing spectacles. Both were sitting in lawn chairs, and both were doing some sort of needlepoint. Right behind them loomed a tall man in a black leather vest. He had a tattoo of a girl in a hula skirt on his left bicep, and below the tattoo was the name "Rosie." He was at the end of the long line, so I fell in behind him.

Almost immediately, a young man wearing shades and puffing on a cigarette fell in behind me. He seemed disappointed that he hadn't been quick enough to beat me to the line.

He had long hair feathered back over his ears and was wearing white pants with a black shirt (popular in the '70s). Behind him a young mother carried a toddler with a runny nose.

"So you guys here for pickles?" I quipped, in an attempt to be both funny and friendly. (It's a curse when your job is being a comedian.)

"Pickles?" said the man with the tattoo, his voice deep and gruff. "Is there a Pickles coming out today?"

"Not that I know of, man," said Mr. White Pants.

They both looked to the young mother with the baby on her hip in hopes that she had heard something about this. She just shrugged and said, "I hope so. I don't have that one."

Tattoo Man frowned, thoughtful. "Me neither."

I chuckled for a moment and then figured I'd better clear this up. "Well, actually, what I meant was—"

But one of the Needlepoint Sisters interrupted. "Pickles?" She held her needle before her as she searched her memory, the needle awaiting a target. "Seems like I heard of that one on CNN."

"Or Fox news," said the other one. "Who does Bernard Shaw work for, anyway?"

No one answered her because Tattoo Man interjected, "Must be a first edition, too!"

"If that's the case . . ." said the other Needlepoint Sister. Her voice trailed off, but she had implied enough so that even Mr. White Pants was able to finish her thought.

"Big bucks, man!"

The talk of big money zipped back and forth and then was slingshot on down the line. Everything was happening too fast. I always had wanted to start a rumor, and now I was seeing one born and grow to adulthood! Even though the situation was funny, I was starting to feel bad and figured I'd better explain. But when I tried ("Really, guys, I just came here for pickles"), Mr. White Pants flicked his cigarette to the ground and crushed it with the toe of his black sneaker, white smoke blowing from his nostrils. I looked to Tattoo Man, but now his eyebrows were bent into a sharp, threatening V-shape above his eyes. His lips were thin and drawn tight. "Rosie" was dancing on his bicep— or at least twitching spasmodically. The Needlepoint Sisters had stopped needlepointing. And I'm pretty sure the way they were holding their needles could have been considered *brandishing*. The young mother just stared at me and gripped her baby tighter. I once read that in some tribes the women have to go into battle. When they do, they tightly strap their infants to their bodies, not only to protect the babies but also to allow the mother to swing a weapon better. Something was very wrong here.

Just then a commotion from at the beginning of the line drew attention away from my pickle problem. From where I stood, I could see the doors were opening.

The Needlepoint Sisters were the first to scamper. They stood simultaneously, kicked back their chairs, and pushed forward in the line. Tattoo Man pushed in close behind them but was pushed back just a bit when one of the women scolded him for his impatience. He blushed, and Rosie turned red. I maintained my place in line and pushed in through the store door just ahead of Mr. White Pants.

Once inside, I was shoulder to shoulder with people looking to get rich quick on animals stuffed with beans—only the focus of most of the talk was now about Pickles—where and how much? My accidental rumor had contaminated the entire room.

"Hey, man, I bet I know!" I couldn't see him, but it was the voice of Mr. White Pants. "Maybe you have to buy a jar of pickles, and then you get a free Beanie."

"*That's* what Bernard Shaw said on CNN!" came another voice I recognized.

"Yeah, that's it!" said anybody and everybody.

In that instant any hope I had for pickles, let alone egg salad, vanished. Tattoo Man cradled at least a dozen jars himself. I watched him waddle to the checkout stand. The Needlepoint Sisters used their skirts as baskets and, between them, carried at least as many as Tattoo Man. The young mother had one in each hand and tried to teach her toddler to hang onto a jar, but the kid had it for only a brief moment before giving it a fling. The jar went airborne in aisle two, hit in aisle three, and splattered all the way to aisle seven. I watched as Mr. White Pants dug through the pickles and glass until he fished out the remnants of the label, shook off the pickle juice, and pocketed what he thought was some sort of entry form. After that, every step of every other shopper began and ended with pickle juice.

It's funny how really great ideas come to you at the oddest times. I did make a purchase that day. After all, David was still going to be hungry at suppertime. But what I bought had nothing to do with pickles. (I didn't want anything to do with pickles for a long time after that, actually.) I paid the cashier and left the store with a smile, my supper in my bag, and my shoes sticking to the tile floor, making a terrible, juicy, squeaking noise with every step.

That night, I brought the water to a slow boil, then added salt and a few strips of bacon, just like I'd seen my grandmother do many times. From the plastic shopping bag I pulled out Bongo, a cute brown stuffed monkey with skinny arms and legs. And with a sharp pair of scissors, I lopped off the little monkey's head and spilled the beans into the now boiling water.

I know I read somewhere in the Bible that "Vengeance is mine saith the Lord." (My mother used to quote it to me again and again and again.) But I couldn't help it. I suppose my smile was more like a smirk as I stood there stirring—slowly and deliberately—and staring into the pot (almost in a trance) until David walked in and sniffed the air. "Mmmm. Are we having beans for supper?"

I nodded and smiled.

"I thought we were having egg salad."

I shrugged. "Couldn't find any pickles anywhere. Hope you're not disappointed."

"No, no. Not at all. You know there's nothing I love more than a good bowl of beans. Don't you know that's my number *one* all-time favorite?"

Yes, I did know that.

I don't think I'll ever get carried away with collecting Beanie Babies. (There isn't enough room in the pantry.)

Anyway, that's how things look from up here.

How to Buy
Gifts for Dummies

When I go to the bookstore and see all those bright yellow books that take up a whole wall, I can't help but feel like such a dummy. I look at some of the titles and think, "I could sure use that." At first I thought the publisher had a really cute idea: Take something complicated (like building a lunar space probe) and explain it in layman's terms. But just the other day I saw *Gardening for Dummies*, *Fishing for Dummies*, *Pregnancy for Dummies*, *Crossword Puzzles for Dummies*, *Bowling for Dummies*, and even *Beauty Secrets for Dummies*.

I've always been too embarrassed to buy any of these for myself. I was afraid the cashier would snicker. So for a while I tried to stay away from bookstores, but that's almost impossible when your husband is an English professor and makes a living reading and writing books.

Then one day, while standing by the bright yellow rows that he so lovingly refers to as "Chonda's own personal reference section" (I didn't laugh), I had this great idea. If I didn't have the nerve to buy them for myself, I should buy these books for people who really needed more help than I did. It would be like finding a Bible verse that I knew someone else really needed to hear—like my husband. So, in a way, buying these books and then giving them away to those in need would be like a ministry. (Isn't it funny how far our minds will go to justify our actions?)

The first book I bought was for my husband.

"A present for me?" he said, pleasantly surprised. He tore open the package to reveal a bright yellow book entitled *Putting the Toilet Seat Down for Dummies*. It was handsomely done with graphs, charts, and illustrations, and David spent a great deal of that evening reading and studying. Every now and then I'd hear him make one of those "Ooh!" sounds of discovery, and he would dog-ear a page so he could find it quickly later. For the next few weeks, I couldn't have been more pleased with the results.

The next book I bought was for our neighbors down the road. It was entitled *Walking Your Dog for Dummies*. I even bought a bookmark with a picture of a cute dog with floppy ears and stuck it in at the beginning of chapter four: "Keeping Your Dog from Relieving Itself in Other People's Front Yards." I wrapped the book up nicely in old newspaper (nothing wrong with just a little hint) and left it on their front porch.

One of the most worthwhile purchases I made was *Making Change for Dummies*. I gave it to the cashier at Kroger's who takes forever to give me my money back, especially if I give him an extra penny to round off the amount, thinking it will make his job easier. After only a few weeks, the book paid for itself in my time alone.

I almost tripped all over myself when I first found *Preaching for Dummies*. I bought two of them (one for my associate pastor, too). This one was chock-full of great chapters like

"Ending a Sermon on Time, Part I," "How to Take Up an Offering Without Sounding Like You're Begging," "How to Take Up an Offering Every Time You Get Together Without Everyone Thinking You're Taking Up an Offering Every Time You Get Together," and my favorite, "Ending a Sermon on Time, Part II." I can't wait until Pastor Appreciation Sunday!

Since I first discovered the value of these books (and how most everyone will benefit from this kindness), I've given away dozens—a small price to pay to change someone's life. I bought *Picking Up Garbage for Dummies* for our garbage collector (mainly for the chapters "How to Keep the Can Standing Upright after You've Dumped the *Entire* Contents into the Back of the Truck" and "What to Do When Some of It Falls onto the Customer's Yard"). I went ahead and bought a couple dozen *Using Your Turn Signal for Dummies* and left a stack of them on the counter at our local Golden Gallon gas station, telling the cashier to give them away to whomever he thought could use one. (I also saved one of those for Mom, only because they haven't yet published *Turning Your Turn Signal Off for Dummies*, but I'm watching.) I gave my brother a copy of *Getting Along with Your Little Sister for Dummies* since we have a family reunion just around the corner.

I was buying books right and left and was starting to think that the world *could* be a better place. I even grew bold enough to buy a book for me: *Making the World a Better Place for Dummies*. Yes, what an exciting new ministry. Everyone around me seemed to be growing and maturing, and sometimes I could just sit and watch them become better people, like watching a rosebud open into a beautiful bloom.

Then one day I received a package in the mail with no return address. I opened it and found one of those bright yellow books, one I hadn't seen before: *Minding Your Own Business for Dummies*.

Ha ha, I thought.

I'm not sure who would have done that. Maybe that fellow at the restaurant, the one I gave a copy of *How to Chew Your Food in Public for Dummies*, or maybe the woman at Kroger's, the one I gave a copy of *How to Prepare All Your Coupons Before You Get in the Checkout Line for Dummies*.

I just stood there staring at the book, mortified—like when someone gives you a verse from the Bible about something you didn't even know you were struggling with. Then I remembered my Bible (thanks to *Verses to Remember for Dummies*): "Why do you look at the speck of sawdust in your brother's eye and pay no attention to the plank in your own eye? How can you say to your brother, 'Let me take the speck out of your eye,' when all the time there is a plank in your own eye? You hypocrite, first take the plank out of your own eye, and then you will see clearly to remove the speck from your brother's eye" (Matthew 7:3–5).

Oh, well, I guess it could have been worse. Someone could have sent me *Comedy for Dummies*.

Anyway, that's how things look from up here.

What Time Is It When the Chickadee Chicks?

It was a dark and stormy night. Okay, it really wasn't stormy. In fact, the night was rather peaceful. Zachary and Chera were sound asleep, and the cat and the dog were curled up on a pillow in the garage. David turned over on his side in our bed and told me goodnight. I lay in the bed with my laptop open, my head propped up with a couple of fluffy pillows that aren't good for anything else, and played FreeCell. David calls my laptop a card machine, but I do quite a bit of computing on it also—when he's not around.

After only a few hands (most of which I won, by the way), I turned off the card machine—I mean, computer—tossed the oversized pillows to the floor, and settled into my sleeping position: on my back, ankles crossed, and covers pulled up beneath my chin. Sigh.

I was close to passing over into dreamland when I saw the flashing red numbers on the clock on the nightstand by the bed.

I opened my eyes all the way. Big, red numbers were flashing twelve . . . twelve . . . twelve. (Just like Mother's VCR.) Then I remembered the power had blinked off earlier in the day, which meant that every clock in the house had been knocked out.

I sat up, swung my legs over the side of the bed, and picked up the clock. In the dark, I traced my fingers along the top and discovered several buttons. I experimented with a number of button combinations until finally twelve . . . twelve . . . twelve stopped flashing. There. Now I just needed to know what time it was.

I know, I thought, *the Weather Channel always has the local time*. So I turned on the TV and watched for a long time, but all they were showing on the Weather Channel were maps of the country with big swirls, and *H*s and *L*s pasted all over the Midwest. A wristwatch was around somewhere, I thought, but it could be in about eight different places, and I didn't want to start tearing the place apart.

Then I did what I always do when I need an answer—just any answer. I called Mom.

"Hello, Mom?" I whispered. "I was trying to set my clock, but I don't know what time it is. Do you know?"

"Oh, honey, are you having trouble sleeping again?"

"No, I'm fine. I just need to know the exact time."

"I'm not sure, honey."

"Well, look at your clock," I said.

"This one doesn't glow in the dark," she said. "I thought it did when I bought it. That's the only reason I did buy it. I may take it back to Wal-Mart tomorrow. I sure need one that glows in the dark for times just like this. I'll exchange it tomorrow."

"When did you buy it?"

"Oh, two years ago, but I've been wanting to take it back for a long time."

"Sorry your clock doesn't glow in the dark, Mom. But can you just turn on the light and tell me what time it is?"

"Oh, darling, Sammy's sleeping so soundly. If I turn on the light, I know he'll wake up. Can't I just call you in the morning, after the sun comes up, and tell you?"

I didn't want to disturb Sammy, my stepfather, but I sure did want to know what time it was. "Well, what about that bird clock I bought you for your birthday? What does it say?"

"It's in the kitchen, and besides, it doesn't work at night."

"What do you mean it doesn't work at night?"

"I mean, it doesn't chirp at night," she explained. "That's so you can sleep without the bird sounds waking you up. But the last bird I heard was an oriole."

"And what time is it when the oriole chirps?"

"Eight o'clock."

"Mom, that was a long time ago."

"I know. We went to bed early."

"Maybe you can go into the kitchen and see what it says."

"The clock?"

"The clock."

"Well ..."

"What is it, Mom?"

"You see, I love the cardinal's song."

"Yes."

"And the cardinal sings at nine o'clock."

"Yes."

"Well, I never seem to be home at nine in the morning because that's when I get my hair fixed on Tuesdays; I have Bible study at that time on Wednesdays; I like to shop then on Thursdays; and on Fridays I like to come over to your place and drink coffee."

"So?"

"So by nine at night, we're usually in bed, and the clock stops chirping. That means I never hear the cardinal. That's why I set my clock up four hours. Or was it *back* four hours? I'm not sure. Anyway, now I can hear the cardinal."

"So I'll just add four hours or subtract. I'll figure it out."

"I may have messed up the minutes, too. As a matter of fact, I'm not even sure I moved it four hours. I just kept turning it until the cardinal sang. I love to hear the cardinal sing—"

"Goodnight, Mom."

"Goodnight, darling."

I had just hung up when the phone rang. "How would you like to have one of those clocks for Christmas?" Mom asked.

So Mom was making a dent in her Christmas list (in February), but I still didn't know what time it was. Now the Weather Channel was showing snowplows pushing through four-foot drifts and cars sliding on icy streets into the backs of other cars. Where was that little time code they always ran at the bottom of the screen?

I looked in three of the places I thought my watch could be, but it wasn't in any of them. So I sat on the edge of the bed, in the dark, and listened to David breathe deeply (not snore, but close). It was so dark, so lonely, so empty, so . . . timeless. *So this is what the middle of the night feels like*, I thought.

I couldn't stand it. I grabbed the telephone and punched in seven numbers—just random numbers. The phone rang four times when someone snatched it up on the other end and growled out a rough, "Yeah?"

"Yes, I'm sorry to call so late—and I know it is *so very late*—but I'm taking a survey and—"

"Lady, do you have any idea what time it is?" he growled.

"No, sir, I don't." I was as matter-of-fact as I could be.

"Well . . . it's . . . it's . . . it's the middle of the night!" Then he hung up on me. Just like that. He was no help at all.

My phone rang immediately, and I picked it up before it could wake David. "Yes?"

Mother whispered, "Honey, I just went into the kitchen to fix myself some water, turned on the lights, and the mockingbird sang me the prettiest song. I'm telling you, you're going to love this for a Christmas present. And, by the way, it's 12:23."

"The mockingbird sings at 12:23?" I asked.

"Oh, no. It sings at seven o'clock. But the clock on my stove says 12:23."

"Thank you, Mother. I appreciate that."

"You're welcome. If you want, I can call you in an hour and let you hear the yellow-breasted, tufted titmouse," she added.

"That's okay. Maybe the next time around."

I went through the house and set all the clocks: the microwave, the oven, the telephone, the fax machine, and finally the clock by the bed. It was 1:00 A.M. before I crawled under the covers. David was officially snoring now, so I turned on the fan and that helped some.

It seemed like I had been asleep for forever when my phone rang again. I answered it. (David just grunted.) "Hello?" I said.

"Honey," Mom said, "I know you said you didn't want to hear the tufted titmouse, but I don't think you really want to miss this." Then I heard lots of whistling and singing, like something you would hear on one of those New Age nature tapes. I could picture Mom in the kitchen, probably standing on a dining room chair and holding the phone up to her bird clock.

"Mom, do you have any idea what time it is?" I asked, once the singing stopped and I listened to what sounded like her climbing down from her chair. Just for effect, I made my voice as gruff as I could.

"Sure I do," she answered. "It's 12:23."

"Twelve twenty-three?"

"That's what my oven says."

Then I realized that's what her oven *always* says. But I wasn't going to let this beat me. And I wasn't going to be ugly like that mean man who had hung up on me. "Mom?" I said.

"Yes, honey?"

"What time is it on your microwave?"

"Well, let's see . . . it says 7:34."

"And the clock on the VCR?"

"Umm . . . it says 6:08."

I paused for a while before caving in. "Mother, does your bird clock have a chickadee song, by chance?"

"Why, it sure does. As a matter of fact, it's coming up next hour. Want me to call you?"

"Sure, why don't you do that."

"I'm telling you," she said, "you're just going to *love* having a clock like this of your own." I could imagine her smiling on the other end of the phone.

I slept very little that night. But I did hear the sounds of at least seven different species of birds before daybreak. I suppose in the midst of the worry about time slipping away, that is a small consolation.

Anyway, that's how things look from up here.

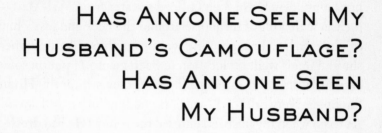

Has Anyone Seen My Husband's Camouflage? Has Anyone Seen My Husband?

Okay, I've gone long enough without saying there are some big differences between men and women. So let me say it now: There are some great big differences between men and women. Whew! I feel better.

After all these years of marriage, my husband is finally starting to buy his own clothes, only everything is green and brown. He says these are the perfect colors when he goes out to the country. Nothing can see him.

I don't understand this. I buy clothes specifically so that someone *will* see me!

"Who is it you don't want to see you?" I asked.

"Not who," he said, "*what*."

"*What* is it you don't want to see you?"

"The live game. You know—deer, turkey."

"Opossums?"

"Naw, I don't care if they see me."

"Then don't dress like the front of a Ford."

"Huh?"

"Just joking."

Sometimes he wants me to go with him to see the gorgeous "game." One day I said I would go. I'm not sure why. I put on my new Kathy Lee Gifford sweater from Wal-Mart—fuchsia with a bit of turquoise around the neck and just a hint of olive woven through. (She wore something like this when she and Regis went on location to Sacramento.) I put on some cute little diamond earrings, the kind they sell on the Home Shopping Network for $2 each, if you buy fifty pair. I was all set to go when my husband entered the room. (He had dressed in the garage.) He looked like a tree—green, brown, drab olive, and fungus-colored.

He took one look at me and said, "You're not wearing *that* are you?"

"What's wrong with this?" I tugged at the sweater and turned around so he could see the back of it as well before he rushed to judgment. "Can't you see the olive?"

"Well, for one, you'll scare off the game."

"What game?"

"The game I hope to see."

"But I thought deer were color blind."

He was looking right at me, but for a moment his mind zipped off far, far away. The wheels inside his head were turning, the way they do whenever I lay down a cold, hard fact that somehow stuck in my head but had gotten past him. I knew what he was doing. He was rewinding every episode of *Wild Kingdom* and *Hunting with Howard and Jim* that he had ever watched on the Sports Channel to find that piece of information. He blinked several times, and that's how I knew he was back.

"Where did you hear that?" he asked. His lips were dry, his breathing ragged.

I shrugged. The wrong answer here could throw him into a state of shock. I recognized the need to withdraw. The wrong answer at this point—something like The Discovery Channel or ESPN II—could have devastating effects. I would have to be careful. So I said, "Oprah."

For the longest moment he stood still. Then a wave of relief washed over his face like rain. He even chuckled. "For a minute there I thought you were serious. Come on, you look good in earth tones. Go ahead and change. I'll be waiting in the Jeep."

My husband doesn't stalk animals to hunt them; he just likes to stalk them for the sake of stalking them. (Wasn't a law passed recently against that? Somebody help me.) Soon we were thick into a jungle of briars and low-hanging limbs. (I was so glad he had talked me out of my fuchsia sweater.) Every so often he would turn to me and point at the ground, where I would see a couple of half-moon tracks grouped close together that were supposed to be hoof prints.

A vision of Elmer Fudd flashed into my mind—not that my husband looks like Elmer Fudd, but remember the episode in which he was hunting for "wabbit," and he looked straight into the camera (what an actor!), and said, "You must be bewrry, bewrry qwiet"?

My husband would point to the track and mouth the words, big and slowly, "Look, deer!"

I would mouth back, "Oh," and nod that I understood, just in case my lips were too hard to read. We did this for five miles.

Point. "Look, deer!"

"Oh." Nod.

Point. "Look, deer!"

"Oh." Nod.

When we finally circled back to the Jeep, I told him how disappointed I was that we hadn't actually seen any deer, just their tracks, but that I was sure some lovely game lived in those woods.

He rubbed his chin thoughtfully and scanned the thicket we had just come from. "Yeah. They can hide pretty good sometimes. I'm not sure what happened. Maybe . . ." he paused, as if considering whether to even mention this tiny maybe, " . . . maybe it was the earrings." He shrugged and opened the Jeep door for me—the bright red, look-at-me-driving-through-the-woods Jeep.

I put a hand to my earlobe and felt the shape of a big, fake, Home Shopping diamond. I started to tell him about a particular episode on a video I'd seen—I think it was a Gary Smalley video. It was about a man who couldn't appreciate that his wife tried to dress herself up for him from time to time, and if that man couldn't hold his woman every now and then and tell her how beautiful she was, then somebody needed to wake up or—but David already was cranking up the monster engine, scaring all the deer deeper into the forest.

Later that night I discovered something about my husband's wardrobe. It is invisible—especially on the floor. I led him through the living room, up the steps, and into the bedroom, every so often stopping to point. I'd mouth the words so he could read my lips. "Look, dear." I pointed to his green-and-brown shirt.

"Oh," he answered with a big nod and then reached down to scoop it up.

"Look, dear," I said, pointing to the green-and-brown socks.

"Oh," and he nodded.

I thought about wearing some camouflage pajamas to bed some night with my handsome Elmer Fudd. If I do, I believe either one of two things will happen: He won't even see me, or—didn't you see that *Oprah* episode?

Did I mention that there are some big differences between men and women?

Anyway, that's how things look from up here.

Why I Love My Cell Phone—Even If I Do Hate It

I have all kinds of reasons to hate my cell phone, but I have one good reason to love it—and, in the end, that reason wins out.

My cell phone and I go back a few years. I remember the very first call I ever made. "Hey, Mom, guess where I'm calling from?" I practically screamed into the mouthpiece, sort of like kids do when they make a telephone out of two cups and a string. The reception was bad, and we could only hear half of what the other person was saying, but we were still giggling and laughing about being able to talk while I buzzed down the interstate at eighty miles an hour. (I was also conducting a legitimate cellular speed test, just in case any law enforcement officers are reading this.) Even now, when I'm driving down the road and my signal starts to break up, I enjoy screaming out, "I'm losing you! I'm losing you!" like one of those doctors on *ER*. That's so fun! But that's not the reason I love my cell phone.

Every now and then, when my husband is lost in the mall, he'll call me from a pay phone and ask, "What women's wear section of which store are you in?" before I can even say hello.

"Let me see," I'll answer. "Are you in the sporting goods section of Sears?"

"How'd you know that?"

"Lucky guess."

"JCPenney has a sporting goods section, too, you know." (He hates being out-guessed.)

Yes, my cell phone is a lot of fun, and it keeps my husband from wandering through the mall all day, calling out my name. But that's not the reason I really love it.

When it rings while I'm in the bathroom, that would certainly be a vote against having one. (I try to change my voice—to talk softly—so the echo won't give me away. But I'm never sure it really works.)

Of course, I have been known to call my mother from the men's restroom. I speak at a number of Women of Faith conferences. They average 10,000 to 15,000 women per event, and no matter how large the arena may be, there are never enough bathrooms for 15,000 women. So, of course, I couldn't resist the legal opportunity to see what the men's room looked like. And, more important, I couldn't resist calling my mother from my cell phone while standing next to the urinals to ask her once again, "Guess where I'm calling you from?" (She never guessed.)

Sometimes the technology of cell phones frightens me. Every year, it seems to get better. They now offer memory, mailboxes, voice activation, built-in phone books, caller ID, and some other features I haven't learned about yet. On my phone, a simple push of one button can connect me to somewhere in Hong Kong.

At least that's what I've always feared ever since I dropped the phone in my purse one day and went to lunch with a friend. When I got home my husband said it was too bad the lasagna had so many onions, and that my girlfriend sure talks a lot. If that's what David overheard, no telling what other people might have heard—other people in Hong Kong! Now, that's an expensive way to reach out and touch someone.

Sometimes my cell phone can embarrass me—or, rather, my husband armed with the cell phone can embarrass me. Once, while waiting for a table in a crowded restaurant in Nashville, David pulled up the antenna and acted as if he were talking with someone. "Yeah, Garth, baby. Listen, I'm sorry about missing our session, but something came up with Elton, and you know how testy he can be when things don't go his way—you know, that candle in the wind sort of thing." I rolled my eyes and tried to move away from him, but he only put one finger in his ear to drown out the crowd and talked louder. "No kidding? . . . That big, huh? Well, make sure you ask for double the Port-a-Potties there were at Central Park . . . That's something. I never knew the pope was a country music fan. Oops. Sorry, Garth, I'm getting a beep. Dolly said she had a couple of lyrics she wanted to bounce off me. I'll get back to you later, GB. Bah-bye." Then he pulled the phone down and said to me, "Dolly can just call back later. Tonight I'm spending quality time with my family. How much longer until our table's ready?" Moments like that, I can do without a cell phone.

The only thing worse than my husband on the cell phone are the times the children try to top their dad for most ridiculous use of the phone. We were driving down the road one night when the deejay announced that anyone coming up with a short song using the words apple, abalone, and anaconda would win a free Michael W. Smith CD. He gave out his station's telephone number, and Chera punched it in. Then she sat with her finger poised over the Send button until she and Zachary could write a song. They came up with one, sung to the tune of "Mary Had a Little Lamb":

Apple, apple, abalone.

Abalone, abalone.

Apple, apple, abalone,

An-a-co-on-da!

They didn't win the CD; they never even got through to the radio station. But they did sing this song for miles and miles, stabbing the redial button over and over. If it hadn't been for the cell phone, we could have enjoyed a pleasant evening drive, discussing family-oriented issues, such as the health risks of having pizza every night during the children's formative years.

And I sure don't keep my cell phone because it's cheap to operate. Once a friend of mine in California called me while I was grocery shopping—in Tennessee. I answered on aisle five, and we talked until aisle twelve, just chitchat really. I felt so guilty about the roaming charges that I put back the imitation crabmeat. That made me feel better.

Yeah, I have lots of reasons to cancel my service—or just to toss the phone in the lake. Life would be easier, slower, and less hectic—although my husband might be lost forever in the mall. But staying "connected" is the main reason I hang onto that blasted cell phone—and I guess it's really the only reason.

Several years ago, I was in Colorado Springs meeting with a number of people about the upcoming Preacher's Kid Conference I host. We were wading through lots of business talk about when, where, how much, who, etc., when my cell phone rang. I took the call while everyone else just held his breath and marked his place so we could resume once I'd hung up.

"Yes . . . yes . . . I see . . . I think that will be just fine. And Miss Terry will bring you home tomorrow? . . . Good. Make sure you take a toothbrush. I love you, and I'll see you tomorrow. Good-bye." I closed up the telephone and looked up. Wide-eyed, inquisitive stares surrounded me. "That was my twelve-year-old daughter asking if she could spend the night with a friend." Everyone still seemed suspended until I added, "I told her it was okay."

Then everyone nodded in agreement as the group lived that moment with me. I patted the cell phone for a job well done. For a moment, at whatever cost or inconvenience, I was connected to my daughter, who was a thousand miles away and wanted my permission to sleep over with a friend. I slipped the phone back into my purse (where there was still the chance it might accidentally dial up someone in Hong Kong), and thought to myself: *In spite of all the problems or embarrassments, the irritation I feel when it rings for the umpteenth time, or the untimely interruptions during my women's prayer meeting, I love that old cell phone.* There's no price too high to pay for staying connected to my children.

Or to my husband. I'm even thinking of getting one for David. For all the quarters he pumps into those pay phones at the mall, it would be worth the investment.

Anyway, that's how things look from up here.

THE DAY MARTHA STEWART
CAME TO MY KITCHEN

I dreamed the other night that Martha Stewart came to my
house for a visit. I knew right away it must have been a dream
because, when she rang the doorbell, it chimed to the tune of
Paganinni's "Fourth Concerto." (Another reason I knew I was
dreaming was because I'd never heard Paganinni's "Fourth
Concerto"—I don't even know if there is a Paganinni—and if
there is, if he ever got past the "Third Concerto.")

When I opened the door, there she was: Martha Stewart,
holding a small package. She smiled at me the way she does
when she's signing off on Sunday mornings and she's whipping
meringue at the same time, kind of bobbing her head. She
looked immaculate, dressed in green and brown earth tones—
so wholesome and fresh. (This made me a bit self-conscious
about the tomato-red terry cloth robe I was wearing.) I noticed
that every hair but one was in place, but when she bobbed her
head once, it fell into its slot. I could only stand there in my

robe, stare at perfection, and wonder why she would come to my house. But, after all, it was only a dream, so I kept sleeping.

"May I come in?" she asked politely.

I shook loose from my trance. "Oh, yes, yes, of course. Excuse me. Come right in." I stepped aside to allow her to pass. I paid particular attention to the brown and green sweater she wore—one I'd seen her weave from silk she herself had harvested on a previous show.

"I love your door chime," Martha said. "It's so inviting. Paganinni's 'Fourth Concerto' has always been my favorite."

"He can sure pick 'em, can't he?" I said. She ignored me.

"Oh, here," she said, offering the package she held. "I made this for you."

I accepted the gift, wrapped in a crinkly blue tissue paper. "You might want to save the paper," she said. "I made it from the bark of a honey locust tree and dyed it with indigo berries." I studied the paper. "It's a good material for making holiday wreaths."

"Can I just reuse it as wrapping paper?"

"And miss out on all the fun of wreath making? But I can show you how to reconstruct the paper. You know, break it down into pulp form and then resize it to the exact dimensions of your gift box, which, by the way, is not all that difficult to construct from the soft core of a balsa tree."

"Wouldn't cut-and-paste be easier?"

She smiled and wagged a finger at me, like a school-teacher reprimanding her first-grade students.

I tore open the package, and some brown stuff that looked like bird seed spilled out everywhere.

"Uh-oh," she said, "you should have opened it a little more delicately. It seems you tore into the scented pillow I created from balsam, cedar chips, and lavender." She sniffed the air. "Doesn't that smell so delicious and inviting?"

I sniffed. It wasn't too bad, sort of like what you smell when you walk past the toiletries section in Wal-Mart.

"Now, go on and open the rest of it," she added.

I peeled back the paper to expose an aluminum-looking fish bowl. I looked at Martha for a clue.

"It's a mold," she said.

"A Jell-O mold?"

"No, no, no." She smiled patiently. "A loaf mold for making salmon mousse."

"Salmon mousse?" I asked. "Is that what we're making?" Martha had no idea what she was getting into.

"With a cucumber sauce," she added. "Come now, lead the way to the kitchen."

It was only three steps away. We could see the dirty dishes from where we stood. But I led anyway.

"Listen, Martha, about this salmon mousse. My kids won't eat anything with salmon in it, and David won't touch anything that's moussed."

"But don't you see?" she said.

"See what?"

"You don't have to *eat* it."

"You don't?"

"Of course not. It just has to *look* good. You do as I say, and you're going to have yourself a nice little salmon mousse. Now, where is your *main* kitchen?"

"This is it." I waved an arm, the terry cloth of my robe flapping like a flag.

Martha surveyed my domain. "I don't see a baster."

"I don't have one."

"Gas oven?"

"Electric."

"Dehydrator?"

"Nope."

"I suppose you have a microwave."

"That I do have."

"That's what I was afraid of."

"And an electric can opener," I added proudly. "The toaster is shot, but as soon as I move my checking account, I'll be getting a new one."

Martha inhaled, the way I imagine her doing in a sea of her native New Jersey flora, searching for the proper berries to create the ink she will use to write her books. "We'll do the best we can," she said.

"Just what are the bricks for?" She pointed to the two bricks I keep stacked in a corner by the washroom.

"Oh, I use those to prop open the windows on sunny days. You know, to let in the fresh air, like you said on that show in which you built an air purifier out of some old bathtub parts." Now that she pointed them out, the bricks did look rather tacky stacked like that. "Do you think maybe you could paint them?" I asked her. "Perhaps tiny murals of the battle of Concord—like the ones you painted on biscuits that can be served for an afternoon tea? That would make them rather *inviting*, wouldn't it?"

"I guess I could do that," she said, staring at the bricks.

Just then David walked in the front door. "Hi, honey," he said to me, giving me a small peck on the cheek. "Hi, Martha," he waved casually, as if he were used to seeing Martha Stewart in my kitchen. "I'll be in the garage," he announced, going out the back door, "working on the Jeep."

"So, where do we start?" I asked Martha.

Martha perused my pantry and after a few moments announced, "If you'll get me some pumpernickel bread, I think we can make this work."

Since this was just a dream, in the very next scene I walked into my kitchen (in clothes—not the terry cloth robe) carrying a bag of pumpernickel bread. Martha was busy at the kitchen sink. She still looked fresh, except for her hair. A few strands in the front had gone awry and lay at a slant across her forehead, like mine sometimes does when I slave over a hot stove all day. She had some freshly chopped vegetables lined up in alphabetical order on the counter: asparagus, beets, carrots, etc.

"How are things going?" I asked.

"We're getting close," she said. "Did you get the bread?"

I pointed to the sack I had set on the counter. "Is that a gas oven?" I pointed to the new contraption in my kitchen.

Martha smiled a kind of smug smile. "Yes. The pinpoint accuracy of a gas oven is a necessity for this recipe, so I took the liberty of procuring one."

"Just *where* did you procure it from?"

"You forgot to tell me you have a gas water heater," she said. "The basic combustion principles are the same as an oven so, with just a few modifications and some basic work with a bench grinder, I produced another small miracle. Martha Miracles, I like to call them."

"You made this oven from my water heater?"

Martha nodded. "Could you hand me the Dijon mustard, please? I'll need it for the cucumber sauce."

Even in my dreams, I sometimes drop things. In one brief moment that little glass mustard bottle slipped right through my fingers and landed at Martha's feet. The impact of the jar hitting the floor blew off the lid and sprayed up a yellow-green substance, painting the front of Martha Stewart's shirt. I'd never seen anything like that happen on any of her shows.

"Oh, my!" I gasped. "Here, let me help." But the more I blotted, the splotchier the pattern became. "I have an idea." I left the room and returned with my big, red, terry cloth bathrobe. "Here, Martha, slip this on, and I'll soak your shirt in vinegar, right?"

"*White* vinegar, please," she said, and in a daze swapped outfits. "The pumpernickel bread," she repeated, her voice even and low. "You did get the pumpernickel bread?"

"Right here." I patted the sack again.

At that moment, Chera and Zachary charged in, just arriving home from school. "Hey, Mom, what are you and Martha Stewart cooking for supper?" Zach asked. In real life he doesn't know who Martha Stewart is.

"Some salmon mousse with pumpernickel bread," I answered, getting more excited about this venture.

"Mmm. Sounds peachy," Zach said. Now I was certain this was a dream.

"Is that pumpernickel bread I smell?" Chera added. "Pumpernickel bread is okay, but I like *chocolate* mousse. Can you substitute chocolate for the salmon? Is it too late?"

I noticed Martha's bottom lip quiver.

"Run along, children," I said. "We'll see what we can do."

"Okay," Zach said. "Hey, maybe we can make some holiday wreaths later!" This idea seemed to excite them both, and they bounded off with great anticipation.

Alone again with Martha I asked, "What about that chocolate idea of Chera's? Any chance we could make a switch?"

Before she could answer, David entered the back door, carrying a fish-shaped Jell-O mold. He laid it in the sink. The inside of the mold was black and oily.

"What have you done to my mold?" Martha asked him, pointing a shaky finger at the mess.

"I just changed the oil in the Jeep," he said. "I borrowed your little fish pan. It worked great." Then David pointed at the oily pan and said, "It's just 10W40. A little bit of that Palmolive stuff will cut right through it. Hey, Martha, you should stay for supper. Then maybe later we could all make some wreaths or something." He walked past me and gave me another peck on the cheek (another reason I knew I was dreaming). "I'll be in the living room watching ESPN," he said. He stopped to survey the kitchen—the twisted metal that was now my new gas oven, the rain of mustard on the floor, the greasy sink—and said to me, quietly so Martha couldn't hear (but she did anyway), "You know, your friend has sure made a mess in here. It's just not, you know . . . *inviting*." And he left.

Martha watched him walk away. She stood there for the longest time, until finally her face flushed crimson, starting at her chin and washing up as if someone had opened up the top of her head and was pouring in a red dye. If this were television and not my dream, I'm sure the producers would have gone to a commercial break at this point. But as I stood there and watched Martha, her face flustered and red (as red as my terry cloth robe she was wearing), her lip quivering, her hair a mess, surrounded by a greasy, disheveled kitchen, I couldn't help but think how much—in my dream—that Martha Stewart looked just like me. Imagine that.

I recently took a trip to Guatemala and visited with Sara, Esparanza's mother. Esparanza is a young girl we sponsor for World Vision. Sara made tortillas on a clay *comales*, a skillet Sara constructed herself (much like Martha Stewart). Every day she grinds corn by hand with a stone to make tortillas—every day, nearly every meal.

As I watched Sara in her filthy cotton dress, squatting on the ground to mold the clay for her *comales*, I could see myself. You see, if the circumstances had been different, had I been born there instead of here, I could be the one preparing tortillas for my hungry family over an open fire and sleeping under a thatched roof.

My kitchen would probably seem like a Third World country to Martha Stewart. Still, when I feel the pressure of trying to be as good a cook as my grandmother, or when the idea of decorating my home so that everything is "inviting" weighs heavily on me, I remember Sara in Guatemala. And I think to myself, *I may be no Martha Stewart, but I'm doing okay. And I am a woman blessed.*

Anyway, that's how things look from up here.

Telemarketers and Other Suppertime Annoyances

I'm convinced that, when we bought our home about a year ago, all those papers we signed at closing were not legal documents at all. They were phone lists. Nearly every evening the phone rings, and it'll be someone trying to raise money for the fire department or the police department, or trying to give me a free family portrait, or sell me cosmetics, or a telephone company trying to outbid all the others. I've received phone calls for everything but a CNN poll; no one's ever polled me about anything.

But you know what I discovered? All these sales people have scripts that go something like this: "Hello. Allow me to introduce myself and the reason I'm calling." (Legally they have to do something like that.) I know these are just people trying to make a living, but I'm trying to eat my pot roast and not comparison shop car insurance at the dinner table.

I have friends who hang up on telemarketers. Others blow whistles into the phone receiver—or do they do that for other annoying calls? I can't remember. But I just can't do that, so I usually ask a lot of questions before the person has a chance to finish his introductory speech.

For instance, the other night someone called about installing a security system in my home. "I just wanted you to know that for a limited time we are offering free installation," the young man said.

"Free?" I asked.

"That's right. We have service representatives in your area right now, and they would be glad to come out and explain the system to you."

"What system?"

"Why, the one we are selling and offering to install for free," he answered.

"How do you know I haven't had one installed already?" I asked, making my voice thick with suspicion.

"I . . . er . . . I don't," he said. "Do you?"

"Why would I tell you that?"

"Because I just want to know if you have one or not—to see if you would be interested in buying one from us."

"How do I know you aren't some cat burglar calling every house in the neighborhood to see who has an alarm system and who doesn't? And as soon as I go to sleep you're going to sneak in and steal everything I own. How do I know that?"

"Well . . ."

"You say representatives are in my neighborhood right now?"

"Yes."

"How many?"

"A couple, maybe."

"What are they driving?"

"I . . . ah . . . I'm not sure."

"*If* you seriously believe I'm so interested in security—and assuming you aren't a cat burglar—then why would you think I'd let a total stranger into my house? What sort of security business are you in anyway?"

"Well ... these are home security systems that—"

"How did you get this number?"

"I ... er ... I'm not sure. It was here when I got here."

"When I say, 'The fat man walks alone,' does it mean anything to you?" I asked.

"Not really."

"Who's Abbie Hoffman?"

"I don't know."

"Where's Jimmy Hoffa?"

"I don't know."

"Was anyone on the grassy knoll?"

"What grassy knoll?"

"And you claim you're in the security business."

"Look, ma'am, perhaps we're not the security service for *you*," he said. "As a matter of fact, I'm taking your name off the list right now."

"What kind of list do you have there, young man?"

"Just a list ... list," his voice cracked on the second list. "But I'm destroying it right now. As we speak. Hear that?" And I could hear the sound of paper being ripped. "All gone. I'm sorry I bothered you."

I softened my voice a little and said, "Hey, I appreciate that. And just between you and me, if anyone asks, this conversation never happened. Okay?"

"Okay."

Then, with a shot of panic I screamed out, "Oh my goodness!"

"What? What?"

"Someone in a dark blue van just drove by," I told him, whispering. "Are your men in a blue van?"

Click.

I know it sounds like a lot of work, but it sure beats letting your blood pressure boil so that you choke on your pot roast. Besides, it entertains the kids. (And, believe me, that's hard to do. They're bored with all my jokes and stories.)

Has anyone ever called to sell you burial plots? They're fun to talk with, too.

"I know this isn't a very pleasant subject to address," the young man who had called said, "but what is even worse is the idea of leaving this entire burden to fall upon your family."

"What do they look like?"

After a long pause he finally asked, "I'm sorry, what do *what* look like?"

"The plots. The burial plots."

"Ah ... well, I'm not sure. Like any other plot, I guess."

"Well, are they grassy?"

"Maybe. Probably."

"Then who mows them?"

"You know, I don't know. I can have a representative come by and explain everything. We have one in the neighborhood right now, and I'm sure he'll have pictures and samples and stuff."

"Do you sell plot covers?"

"Covers?"

"Yeah. I don't want my plot to get all muddy and nasty. I'd like to keep it covered and dry. You know, in case people should come to visit after church, and they're wearing their good shoes."

"I've never had anyone ask about covers before," he said. "But I can check on it for you."

"That's okay. Let me ask you this: If I buy a plot now, can I use it *before* I die? You know, to have picnics, family reunions, things like that."

"I-I'm not sure. It's just a plot—in a cemetery. And I don't think it's very big."

"How far apart do the stakes have to be in a game of horseshoes?"

"I don't think the plots are *that* big."

"Then maybe I should buy several—end-to-end though, not side-by-side," I added.

"I think I can do that." But he didn't sound too sure.

"Do these plots come with a guarantee?"

"Guarantee?"

"Yeah. Like if I buy a beautiful, grassy, sunny spot and I die, how do I know you won't bury me somewhere else, like next to a toxic waste dump or something?"

"We don't bury people, ma'am. We just sell the plots."

"Do you sell a lot of plots?"

"I think we sell a lot of plots."

"How many plots in a lot?"

"I don't know. A lot?"

"Maybe not."

"Uh . . . listen," he sounded more frustrated than ever. "I can send a representative right over, and he can answer all your questions."

"About those representatives . . ."

"Yes?"

"When things get kind of slow around there . . ."

"Yes?"

"They don't like, you know, *hurry* things along, do they?"

"If you are implying that they—"

"Oh my goodness!" I shouted.

"What? What?"

"Someone in a dark blue van just drove by," I told him, whispering. "Is your man in a blue van?"

Click.

Oh, yeah, those calls in the evening can get a bit annoying. But, like I said, *I* never, ever hang up on anyone.

Anyway, that's how things look from up here.

How Our Family Stays Close with the "Find the Phone" Game

We have three cordless telephones at my house, on three separate lines, and no single receiver is ever where it should be. For a long time I would ask everyone, "Please put the phones back where they go when you are finished using them." But I might as well have said, "Clean up your rooms." We are a mobile family. When we talk, we walk, we saunter, we pace. For heaven's sake, I can wash two loads of laundry, put on a roast for supper, and dust the living room furniture during just one conversation with my mother! So in this family (me included), when we finish talking, we're usually miles from where we started—and so is the phone. *That's* why we had a family meeting.

One night we gathered around the kitchen table, and I explained to everyone a new game we were going to play. I said to Zachary, my nine-year-old son, "Zachary, you cover the upstairs."

"How come I get the upstairs?"

"Because you're young and quick. If you slip on the steps, you'll probably just bounce back up," I told him. "Something on your father or me would break."

"But the *whole* upstairs?" he asked. I considered this for a moment, and I realized that I was asking a lot since three bedrooms, one bath, and an office are up there.

"Well," I amended, "everything except Chera's room. And Chera, you take care of that." Chera is fifteen and has lots of clothes—most of them on the floor. Once we lost a phone for two weeks in there.

"But, Mom," Chera protested, "by myself? I could sure use some backup. What's Dad going to cover?"

"I'll cover the garage," David spoke up.

"Nobody ever takes a phone into the garage," Chera said.

"So the odds are just getting bigger that one day someone will," David defended his position.

"Okay," I interrupted. "David, you take the living room, the laundry room, and the downstairs bathroom."

"I have a bathroom, too, Dad," Zach sang. David gave him a high five.

"I'll take the den and the kitchen," I said, scanning the room for any objections. "Now, here's how we play. Wherever we happen to be, or whatever we happen to be doing, when we hear the phone ring, disperse."

"What does *disperse* mean?" Zach asked.

"It's a verb," David answered, "meaning 'to drive off' or 'to send off in various directions; to scatter.'"

"Oh," Zach said. "That sounds fun." (Zach has to work on his sarcasm.)

"Anyway," I continued, "remember your zones. On the cue—which is a ring—cover your zones and try to pick up before the answering machine kicks in."

"And if we don't make it?" Chera asked, her voice thick with concern.

I took a deep breath and answered, "Then we clean our rooms—*everybody*." We all exchanged glances, suddenly feeling the gravity of the situation. Already, I could sense we were pulling together as a team. "Any questions?" Silence. "Can we do this?" I asked, my voice rising a bit.

I scanned each and every face. Zach bit his lip and nodded. Chera took a deep breath and blew out, then nodded. David squinted, as if he were adding up numbers (odds maybe), and finally he nodded. "Okay, then," I said. "Everybody, hands in the middle." I'd seen Zach's Little League team do this before games. "Find the phone on three. Ready? One, two, three—"

"FIND THE PHONE!!"

I truly believed in this group. It was a proud moment for me.

A few days went by without incident. Everyone seemed conscientious of the phones and their distance from their respective cradles. Chera would answer and just plop herself down on the floor and talk—no more roaming. Zach refused to take calls altogether. "If it's for me," he said, "I'm not here." (I don't think it was ever for him.)

But eventually it did happen, as we all knew one day it would. The phone rang, and it was nowhere to be found. I stared at the empty cradle through two whole rings before screaming out, "PHONE!!"

You should have seen my family move. Zachary flew past me in a blur, up the steps, looking in nooks and crannies for a phone that shouldn't be there but possibly could be. The sound of thunder came from Chera's room, and I could picture her throwing things from one side of her room to the other, searching for a phone that shouldn't be there but possibly could be. As I looked into the living room, I saw cushions fly, I saw David fly, and I saw the telephone fly by. It split the air with ring number three just as it went past me and landed in the open clothes hamper at the door of the laundry room. Still technically in

David's zone, but . . . I seized the phone and called out, "Got it!" Then in the middle of ring number four, just before the answering machine could come on, I pressed the talk button. "Hello," I said. "Yes . . . Yes . . ." It was for me, but my family surrounded me anyway, sweating and panting and collectively proud of their accomplishment.

"Just what do they look like?" I said into the receiver. "Why, the burial plots, of course . . . yes . . . yes, I see . . . grassy? Good . . ."

We have a lot of fun at our house with "Find the Phone." Just about everywhere I go, I suggest it as a wholesome family activity. Still, even though this is a fairly wide-open and spontaneous fun time, we have learned a few things that can make "Find the Phone" that much more enjoyable—and safe—yet will not take away from the hours of pleasure your family is sure to experience.

1. The more cordless phones you have, the more fun you are guaranteed. Many times when we played, someone would call out, "Got it!" only to realize it was a different line ringing. When this happens, just laugh and keep on searching.

2. It's best not to play this game in stocking feet—especially if you have wood or vinyl flooring. Once David took a corner too wide through the kitchen and collided with the refrigerator. The refrigerator was okay, but just about all the magnets on the front were ruined.

3. I'd suggest that only one person yell out "PHONE!" because with all the yelling, you waste valuable search time. And remember, this is a team sport, so name-calling is uncalled for.

4. Don't show off by flipping the telephone like a gunfighter if you find it first. Those stubby, rubber antennae can put out someone's eye. David wore his patch for three days.

5. Never, *never* hide the telephone intentionally, setting yourself up to be a hero the next time it rings. The garbage disposal wasn't even in Zachary's territory to begin with.

I don't know where I get these ideas. Probably from my mother. She was always trying to take an aggravating situation and make something fun out of it. Once, when I was a kid, we didn't have any eggs to dye for Easter, so we painted rocks. I wish you could have seen her face when we actually saw something like that for sale at a craft shop years later. She went on and on about how we should have kept those rocks because they would be priceless antiques by now.

So why not go ahead and lose your phones and divide up your territories? Make something fun out of the aggravation.

What was that? Did I just hear a phone ring?

Anyway, that's how things look from up here.

WHAT ARE A FEW MINUTES BETWEEN FRIENDS?

Something that's been on my mind lately is a conversation I had with my husband about time—more specifically, about being on time. Sometimes I think he obsesses about it. But, then again, I usually never know what time it is because my Minnie Mouse watch is broken (just one hand, really—the short one), and the clock on the microwave is still flashing 12:00. But, then again, why should I bother with time when I have a husband who obsesses about it?

"Okay," David said, his face lathered up, pointing a Schick at me as we stood before the bathroom mirror. It was Friday night, and we were getting ready to meet some friends for dinner. "Let's go over this again. Suppose you have an appointment at six, and you're trying to figure out what time you should leave the house so you won't be late."

"Okay. A.M. or P.M.?" I asked.

He thought for just a moment and then said, "That doesn't matter; this is just an example."

"Excuse me," I protested, "but it most certainly does. Because, if you're talking A.M., that's not going to happen. I'll cancel that one in a heartbeat. No friend of mine would ask me to meet her at 6 A.M.!"

"Okay, P.M. then," he said. "You will need to estimate your LT—leave time. Say it takes twenty minutes to get there from here. That means you will need to leave the house no later than 5:40."

"That sounds easy," I said. "Just simple math, right?"

He held up his hand to stop me. "That's not all. Suppose you make *one* wrong turn. You drive two-and-a-half minutes before you realize your mistake, so then it takes you two-and-a-half minutes to come back to where you started. That's five whole minutes. But if you *pad* your trip with some extra time, just in case something like that happens, you'll still be on time. So, all you have to do is factor that into your LT—your leave time—which would now be no later than 5:35 P.M."

I thought about that for a minute and then asked, "Is this some place I've been to before?"

"Maybe."

"Then I won't make a wrong turn, so give me my five minutes back."

"Okay, say it's somewhere you've never been before, and you get so lost you spend forty-five minutes driving around in circles before you find the right street." He rinsed his razor and smiled at me, as if he had me this time.

"I'll stop to ask directions," I said, "which won't take more than one minute."

He still saw this as a victory for him and exclaimed, "Aha! So you admit that you need to leave the house by no later than 5:39?"

"Sure."

"Good," he said, shaving the underside of his chin. "Now we're getting somewhere. Suppose," he continued, "that you need some cash. So you zip through the Anytime Teller Machine. Six minutes, minimum."

"Six?"

"Have you memorized your secret number yet?"

"No, but it's in my purse."

"And will you be taking *that* purse?" he pointed to my "larger" purse by the door. I nodded. "Then you'd better allow *eight* minutes. That brings us back to leaving the house no later than 5:31."

I thought for a moment, feeling like maybe he had me there. "Yeah, but I keep all my credit cards in the big purse," I said, "so I won't need the cash. Now give me back at least four minutes." I could tell he was becoming a bit frustrated—the nicks on his chin gave it away. "I'm not going to use up all my time on cash machines and getting lost," I protested. But since he seemed to be losing a lot of blood, I decided to go along with him—just to show him how silly his idea was. "So now what?"

"Okay. What if you have a flat tire?" he said, pressing a tiny piece of tissue to a spot on his chin.

"Then I'll call Triple A and take a cab, but that's no more than five minutes."

He smiled. "Good. So we agree on leaving the house no later than 5:37 then, right?"

"Okay."

"And what if they've closed a lane to work on potholes?"

"Maybe fifteen minutes," I said.

"That's what I was thinking." He was almost pleasant about this exchange now. "So 5:22?"

"Sure. And what if there happens to be a parade that day?" I added. "You know, St. Patrick's Day, Thanksgiving—"

"Or some astronauts just getting back from the moon!" he said. He was serious. "Yeah, that could happen. So take away another ten minutes for the detour, and we're at 5:12. And what," the sudden thought just came to him, "if, on the detour route, a giant sinkhole has opened up in the middle of the street! You're not going to get around that in less than twenty minutes because of all the emergency trucks, CNN camera crews, and gawkers. That's 4:52 now."

"Better make it 4:47," I added, "because I'd probably take another five minutes to hop out and take a look at the sinkhole myself, since I've never seen one either."

He nodded with understanding. "Okay. So now we're at 4:47. This is good. I think you're beginning to understand what it is I've been talking about. What else?" he asked, seeming to respect my opinion about what could go wrong.

"Well, a bank could be robbed, and the police would set up roadblocks at strategic points," I said.

David applied a couple more tiny pieces of tissue to his nicked face and said, "Yeah, I never thought of that. But we'd better allow for *two* roadblocks. Always have to be prepared." Then, with a great deal of concern, he looked at me and said, "I'm worried about you out there with those bank robbers."

"I'll be okay," I said. "I'll even have the police check the trunk both times."

He nodded. "Good. Let's allow thirty minutes each time; so there's an hour. That means you need to leave the house no later than . . ." he squinted while he figured, " . . . 2:52."

"That's easy enough to do," I said. "For sure, I'll be there by six."

He smiled. But just as quickly, it dissolved into a frown. "I'm forgetting one thing, though."

"What's that?"

"Have you ever had your appendix removed?"

I shook my head. "I don't think so."

"Hmm. So there's always the chance it could rupture en route."

"Well, yeah. And there's always a chance I could win the American Family Publisher's sweepstakes and Ed McMahon would want to ask me a few questions—you know, for next year's commercial."

"Oh, I hadn't thought of that," said David. "Okay then, to allow for any hospital stay or TV time (which would include makeup and wardrobe, etc.) you probably should leave . . . two days early."

"*Two days!?*"

"I'm sure most of that time would be down time—filling out insurance forms, things like that."

"I live twenty minutes from this hypothetical meeting, but you're saying I should leave two days early?"

"The time passes fast. So what if you're a bit early? Just do what I do."

"What's that?"

"Walk around Home Depot for a few hours."

"Great."

"The important thing is that you have some padding built in for any sort of emergency," he said. "If you establish a habit of this sort of contingency planning, you'll never be late again." He smiled smugly, but then exclaimed, "Oh, my goodness! What time is it?"

I checked the bedroom clock and said, "A couple of minutes before six."

"5:58?! Aren't we supposed to be at the Jackson's at 6:30?" He was on the verge of panic.

"Relax. We can be there in ten minutes."

"Not if your appendix ruptures," he said, as serious as he could be.

"You're the one who's going to need blood, if you keep cutting yourself that way," I said. He brushed off the tiny pieces of red-spotted tissues, and we dressed and rushed out the door in record time.

"I hate being late," David said, backing out of the drive.

"We'll just tell them we were abducted by a UFO," I joked.

But David wasn't smiling. "I never thought of that, either," he said. And I could see the little math wheels in his head turning.

We made it to our friends' house with plenty of time to spare. As we walked up to the porch, we noticed everything seemed rather dark. "Usually Philip has the grill already going by this time," David said, ringing the doorbell.

"And Angela's pouring the tea," I added.

David checked his watch again. "We're on time, I tell you," he said proudly. "It's 6:30 on the nose."

We waited longer than we should have and rang the bell more times than we should have before turning to leave. While David was tapping on the face of his watch and we were walking slowly back to the car, it suddenly occurred to me what had happened. "Okay, David," I said. "Say you're supposed to meet some friends for dinner on *Saturday*, and you need to calculate your CMD—that's the correct meeting day—by at least glancing at the calendar on *Friday* . . ."

Anyway, that's how things look from up here.

I Could Have Been an Entrepreneur, If It Hadn't Been for All That Business Stuff

I jumped in a cab in St. Louis one morning and headed for the airport. Just as the taxi pulled onto the interstate, three Canadian geese waddled across the entrance lane, and the cab driver had to swerve to miss them. (He also yelled out a few colorful words—a detail I think I'll choose to leave out of this story.) St. Louis may be the home of the Cardinals (you know, Mark McGuire stuff and all), but it's also the home of hundreds—or is it thousands—of Canadian geese. And when you get that many geese together, there's going to be trouble.

"Can you believe," said the cab driver, "that someone is making money riding around in a golf cart with a Shop-Vac strapped in the back and cleaning up goose poop from public parking lots and walkways?"

"Really?"

"That's right," he said. "Some smart entrepreneur is really cleaning up. No pun intended. But I guess it's worth whatever he gets paid. He really found a niche there. No pun intended."

I decided to limit my comments for fear the conversation would surely digress. But I couldn't help but think to myself, *If he—this smart entrepreneur—was working a regular old nine-to-five job, the people of St. Louis would still be watching their step. So he does good, for himself and for the people he lives with. But isn't there a better way to make a living? Could he really be happy with a Shop-Vac?*

Anyway, this smart entrepreneur has inspired me, and I've been keeping my eyes open just in case one day I'm not funny anymore, and I have to get—in the words of my mother—a "real job." It's important to me that I find a job I really like, and one that helps people—like that guy's in St. Louis. I'm sure when he heads out in his golf cart with his vacuum cleaner, he feels good about clearing off the walkways so people don't have to worry about their new sneakers. That's why I've been keeping a thumb on the pulse of women today—watching and listening and trying to come up with ideas.

Let's face it—once in a while we all get a little tired of our jobs. Don't get me wrong; what I do seems to have meaning most of the time. Still, some days the golf cart job doesn't sound so bad—especially those days when the thought of climbing on one more airplane makes me want to scream.

So far, I've thought of a few good alternatives. (Actually, the first one was David's idea. He says he was inspired.)

Does your mother-in-law call frequently? Or at least once a month? Do you have to force yourself to pick up the phone when you recognize her number on the caller ID? Then how about We'll Talk to Your Mother-In-Law for You, Inc.? For a small fee, you can have your mother-in-law's call forwarded straight to our bank of professionals, who will respond from a script you have provided. Or leave the details to our trained professionals, who can draw from their vast knowledge of dealing with mothers-in-law (which means most of the time they would probably say something like, "Yes, Mom. You're absolutely right"). Our charge: a whole lot less than the million dollars it would be worth.

Or how many times has *this* happened? You've spent most of the day at the store, wrestling brightly colored boxes from your infant who can't read yet, but who has seen the commercials so he wants to open the box to find the dirt bike that does wheelies over the cereal flakes. At last you think you've reconnoitered everything you'll need to make that surprise recipe for supper you've been dying to try, only to find, when you get back home, that you've forgotten the bottle of dill. AARRGG! Don't worry. Just call We'll Go to the Store for You Even Though You Just Got Back from the Store Yourself, Inc. For a small fee, we will let you stay at home, where you will be more valuable wiping oatmeal off the TV screen and removing the diaper your toddler has managed to put on the family dog. I could have used this type of service dozens of times myself, and I would gladly have paid big bucks for it.

What if your only job for the day was to get the oil changed in the family van? It takes fifteen minutes, right? But that's under ideal conditions, not when the carpet cleaner, the alarm installation man, and the man who wants to spray a green chemical on your lawn ("So you'd better keep the kids indoors for a few days—if ya know what's good for 'em") all show up at the same time. Just go to Oil Change Sticker Service, Inc., where you could buy several blank oil-change stickers those oil change places put on your windshield. Simply hide them in the junk drawer, and then, when you need them, you could fill in the information and stick it to the window yourself. When your husband gets home, he won't feel the need to remind you about the "one and only thing" he asked you to do for the day. (I would also make the customer sign a waiver that states these stickers are only temporary, and that Oil Change Sticker Service, Inc. is not responsible for whatever car parts may fly off due to contaminated oil while cruising down the interstate.) At the least, I think this service would keep peace in the house for a few days.

Then there's that business we all hate to face: when your husband comes home expecting some fancy, schmancy spread on the table (some husbands still live in the '50s), and you have to look him in the face and say, "Looks like leftovers tonight, dear." How much would you pay to have someone else say it? Well, I thought up a pretty good deal, I believe, with Looks Like We Have Leftovers Tonight, Dear, Inc. For a small fee, we would send over a trained professional to break the news to your family. For an extra two bucks (cheaper than extra topping on a large pizza), you would get your choice of the meek girl-next-door, the brash woman with an attitude (one of my favorites— and probably the most requested), a rock band that plays its own instruments, a Mafia boss, or even a ventriloquist act (who breaks the bad news while drinking a glass of water). I foresee this as a business that would grow and change as society grows and changes. Eventually, I would love to add some jugglers, maybe an animal act or two, even someone in the martial arts field.

Oh well, it's good to know that if the comedy ever gives out, I'll have something to fall back on. All of these opportunities are good, honest (the blank oil change stickers being questionable) businesses I believe would succeed, solely because when women get up to their eyebrows in "stuff," they'll pay anything to anyone just "to take care of it." Just like when men *forget* "stuff," they'll pay anything to anyone just "to take care of it." That's why I was thinking of branching out into other businesses that would appeal to men, such as Pay Her a Compliment Without an Ulterior Motive, Inc. or perhaps something like We'll Make the Plans for You So You Can Look Spontaneous, Inc. I wonder if anyone's ever thought of selling flowers in a hardware store? I could call it Roses and Hoses. I just might get rich!

Anyway, that's how things look from up here.

Is There a Gardener in the House?

The only reason I took up gardening was because I like flowers. I don't like gardening—just flowers. Maybe I wouldn't mind gardening so much if it weren't for all that digging and mulching. Maybe what I really need is just a flower shop, where everything comes in already grown and blooming, thus skipping the watering and weeding.

Even though I complain, I have gained a greater appreciation for my old biology professor, John Dix, who knew every species of flower you can imagine (even the Latin name for crabgrass). I do feel bad that it has taken me twenty years to gain this appreciation—maybe it would have helped me pass the course back then.

What I've learned recently is that a pickax and a spade axe are not the same thing. I've also learned that a froe is a heavy, sharp, digging object on a stick, and that it's about the only thing that cuts through the clay stuff in my backyard. I've also learned to wear gloves all the time (except when you spill lemonade on your chin and you want to wipe it off), to never wear sneakers if you plan on doing a lot of digging with a shovel, and that earthworms have more than one heart and will grow back if you whack them in two (so there's no need to pray for each one you slice, dice, or quarter).

I began to learn all these gardening things at the beginning of spring, when I first plotted out the land. Initially, I envisioned an acre of poppies, an acre of wild daisies, and an acre of dahlias. That was before I learned how big an acre was. So I settled for a tiny patch—a six-foot square patch, to be exact— of wildflowers.

"Wildflowers are nothing more than weeds that bloom," David told me. "*Anyone* can grow them." (David was showing off his *Jeopardy* skills more than he was trying to insult me.)

First, my husband told me we had to prepare the soil. But our backyard is not really soil; it's clay. When it rains, you tie a rope around your waist if you visit the backyard so someone can pull you back in when you get stuck. (Just like something out of the Old Testament—you know, like when the priest would tie a rope around his waist before visiting the Holy of Holies. Okay, maybe not.) And when it's dry, the soil is like digging on a dinner plate; the shovel makes the same sound as a fork scraping some of that stoneware we eat off of. It seemed pretty clear that if I wanted something to actually grow, I needed to go across the street and buy topsoil at the nursery.

Anyway, I dug up my little square for wildflowers (not quite the six-foot square I had hoped, more like four-foot), dropped in $2.50 worth of seeds, mixed it with $50 worth of dirt, and waited for beauty to spring forth. I didn't care if they were weeds; the picture on the front of the packet was the same floral design as in my bathroom. I took that as a sign of affirmation.

"Looks like most of this will germinate in seven to ten days," David said, reading the empty seed package.

"Seven to ten days!" I blurted. "But I want to see some flowers now! I thought you said these were like weeds. Weeds grow overnight! Haven't you heard the expression, Grow like a weed? I don't have the time or patience to wait seven to ten days."

"Oh, I was wrong," David added, still reading. "You won't have to wait seven to ten days for your flowers, after all."

"Thank goodness."

"That's the germination time. They won't bloom for four weeks."

Despite my discouragement, I was going to stick with my flower bed. I would not be denied those pretty blue asters. So I watered them—or at least I watered the dirt. Exactly a week later, green shoots began to pop up all over. I was so excited I knelt down in the dirt and touched each one, as if they were my little babies.

"Oh, I wonder what *this* is?" I said, gingerly bending a tiny shoot—which was the largest of the little shoots—first one way then the other.

David leaned on his shovel and spit away from me. (I don't know why men think they should spit when they are working outside in the dirt.) He said, "Hard to say when they're so young. Could be a beautiful sunflower." He spit again. "Or it could be one of those obnoxious chigger weeds that we'll lop off later. You never know what they'll grow up to be."

"Well, *this* one's a sunflower," I said, determined. "And I will raise it as such. And I will love it." Then I stepped quickly to the side, realizing I was blocking its sunlight. Oh, the horrors I went through that night, believing it could have been choking and gagging, desiring its chlorophyll, but being blocked off from its sustenance by my big, bulky shadow.

The spring was nice. We had lots of rain, so the ground stayed moist and soft. My little shoots began to grow, and the one I had spotted so early in the season was proving itself to be a legitimate wildflower—what kind we still weren't able to tell. Once a week, I kept my little four-foot square hoed, imagining the tiny shoots saying, "Thank you for the cultivation. We can breathe so much better now."

"You're welcome," I would answer them.

Then one day tragedy struck: I got a little too close while wielding my hoe and whacked down what looked like a zinnia. At first I tried to stick it back on. Maybe it would heal itself up before it lost too much green juice—like the earthworms. I balanced the severed half on what was left of its tiny stalk, but it kept tipping over. And the Scotch tape didn't work, either; the stalk was too hairy. I pronounced the little plant dead and buried it in the same spot where it had once thrived.

David tried to make me feel better. "It'll make more room for the others," he said. "Believe me, they'll all be better off because of it." Gardening seemed so cruel.

To be honest with you, before they ever had a chance to bloom, when it still looked like just a weed patch I was cultivating and watering everyday, when I still couldn't tell the good guys from the bad guys (and the last thing I wanted to do was to spend half my summer growing a milkweed you can find on the side of the highway), I got a little tired of it all—the hoeing, the watering, the talking, and the fertilizing ("p-yoo!").

So I began to hoe only half of my four-foot square and let the other half turn to pottery. And I let the weeds overtake what I thought were wildflowers. (If wildflowers are nothing but weeds, I learned that there are meaner weeds out there without blooms.)

Why is it that something as valuable and beautiful as a flower needs so much care and cultivating, but weeds don't? If you wanted to plant a weed garden, I think the instructions on the seed packet would read, *"Toss seeds onto the ground. Neglect and step on seeds as much as possible. Germination time: one minute. Thorns, stickers, and safe nesting area for ticks, chiggers, and snakes will take longer—maybe a day. For added attraction, park an old car or stack some old lumber on top of your newly planted weed bed and watch how fast your plants will grow. Disclaimer: Property value could be reduced by the use of these contents."*

By the time July came along, I had all but abandoned my gardening project. My hoeing area had shrunk to the little square where I had found my first, tiny, green shoot. I couldn't bring myself to leave it unattended. By mid-August, I was working the soil around my plant with a spoon and watering it with a cup. All around me, as I worked, loomed big, green leafy things with thick stalks. I continued to talk to my small plant, which was developing its own nice, fleshy leaves by now and carried a cute little pod at the end of its skinny stalk. Inside that pod, I knew, was a bloom. I was more determined than ever to stave off those thorny intruders. I borrowed David's weed whacker and knocked them all down, laying them out like so many giants upon the hard ground. (Bringing to mind yet another Old Testament story.) The next day, they returned— not leaking any green juice and not hurt a bit. But my single plant and I stood our ground.

Then one day I noticed something that nearly made me weep. Way back in the tangle of the thick weed bed I noticed a bright yellow spot of color. I slipped on David's big leather gloves and pushed back the stalks until I could tell it was a single daisy, standing upright and blooming proudly in the midst of its callused neighbors. Immediately, I got out my pruning shears and began to lop off the trunks of the enemies. With more determination than I had ever had so far, I cleared a path to the daisy and then cut a circular swath around it, until it stood alone in the center of a small clearing. I stood there for the longest time, sweating, panting, my arms scratched and bleeding, partially dehydrated, just staring at the daisy. It was beautiful. I loosened the soil around its roots and brought it a cup of water.

Later that week, my sunflower opened up. It was a miniature plant, no taller than my waist, but the design and pattern were gigantic. I stared at it for hours and hours over the next few days. For what remained of the summer, I had *two* flowers: One I had nurtured from a seed; the other I had rescued from its enemies.

I can remember the blisters, the sweat, the aching muscles, and the odor of manure only if I try really hard. None of them is so overwhelming that I can't force it from my mind. But the beauty I saw in those two simple flowers, my sunflower and my daisy, is stamped in my mind more permanently than an Elvis poster at the post office.

I guess I can look at this experience a couple of ways. One, I worked hard—on a small scale—and, by a miracle of God, grew beauty in soil that otherwise would have been good for nothing but cooking tacos on. That thought crosses my mind quite a bit. But it's the other thought that gets into my brain and worms its way around like an earthworm that just won't die: What if I had hoed and watered the whole area all summer? What if I hadn't gotten discouraged? Would there have been more of those perfect daisies, or something even more spectacular? What if I had worked even if I hadn't felt like it? What if I had set my sights on those blooms whose color knocks you out rather than be slowed down because of a shovel of stinky fertilizer? What if....

And that brings a final thought from the Bible to mind: "Let us not become weary in doing good, for at the proper time we will reap a harvest if we do not give up"(Galatians 6:9).

Anyway, that's how things look from up here.

Finding Our Common Ground Off-Road

Sometimes when I'm at the mall, I'll spot married couples walking hand-in-hand, and that makes me smile. Other times, I'll watch them enter together and observe how she goes one way and he goes another, and their paths seldom cross. I would be foolish to think that married couples should do *everything* together. But it's no more foolish a notion than married couples who never try to do *anything* together. I recently learned that, no matter how distant you may feel from your spouse in the area of likes and dislikes, a closer look can often reveal some unrealized common ground—like the time David taught me the Jeep wave.

David had wanted a Jeep since he was a kid (but then again he's always been a kid). Like a kid he would whine, "This is all I'll ever want for the rest of my life. I don't want any candy, or toys, or vacations to Disney World. This is for the rest of my Christmases and birthdays for my whole life. I promise I won't ever ask for anything else."

Like the pushover I am, I gave in. So David picked out a tomato-red Jeep Wrangler with big silver wheels. On the drive home, I watched him adjust the mirrors and push all the buttons that really are buttons and everything else that just looks like a button. He was in his own little world over there behind that wheel. But that was okay; now the minivan was all mine.

Then he did something kind of odd, something I'd never seen him do before. Each time we passed another Jeep on the road, he raised one hand as if he were about to tip his cap, but instead, he gave a choppy wave with two fingers while he gave a quick little nod.

"What's that all about?" I asked, after the third wave.

"What?" He seemed a bit embarrassed. So I tried to re-enact his little gesture.

"Oh, that? It's a Jeep wave," he said.

"A Jeep wave? Where did you learn that?"

He shook his head. "You don't learn it; you just *know* it. All Jeep people know it. See." And he pointed to an oncoming Jeep. The driver waved, just like David had earlier. David waved back. "Pretty cool, huh?"

"Kind of silly, if you ask me. I mean, you've only been a Jeep person for ten minutes."

"Real Jeep people are Jeep people from the time they're born. Some of them just don't know it yet."

"How about me? Am I a Jeep person?" (It really didn't matter to me whether I was or I wasn't.)

He studied me for a moment before saying, "I don't think so. I think you're more a minivan person."

I knew that already. "Oh, yeah?" I said. "Then how come I don't know the minivan wave?"

"Because," he grinned, as if he couldn't believe the answer wasn't as obvious to me as it was to him, "minivan people don't wave. They just poke along and stop every now and then to pick up more neighborhood kids to take to ball practice."

Just then another Jeep passed us, and I offered a good, solid Jeep wave. Nothing to it. David looked at me sternly. "It's not nice to fake a Jeep wave," he said.

For the next couple of days, David spent a lot of time washing, rubbing, and admiring his Jeep. (I think I even caught him practicing his Jeep wave in the garage.) He was wiping a speck of dust off the grill when I came up from behind. "So," I asked, "when are we going to take that bad boy off-road?"

He stopped buffing and looked at me. "What do you mean by 'off-road'?"

I couldn't help myself. "You know, off the asphalt and into the mud, sludge, and grit of the outdoors."

"I . . . ah . . . I'm not sure. Why?"

"Just had an urge, I guess."

"Are you making fun of me?"

I smiled warmly. Of course I was. But I said, "Of course not, darling. It's just that sometimes I get so cramped up in that little minivan that I'm ready to burst out into the wide-open outdoors."

"You're making fun of me." He turned away and began to rub down the front grill some more.

"Oh, just one thing," I said. "I need to run to the store for a few items. Do you mind if I take the Jeep?"

Silence.

"I'll be careful. I promise." I don't know why I like to tease him like this.

"You won't take it off-road, will you?"

"Of course not," I said, taking (pulling) the key from his hand. As I drove away, I watched him in the side mirror, appearing farther away than he actually was. He was clutching his buffing towel and staring at me driving away. He didn't even give me a Jeep good-bye wave.

We live in a subdivision that is still growing and still subdividing. At one end, workers are framing, plumbing, and putting underground whatever it is that requires them to dig four-feet-deep holes. All the dirt is located on that end of the subdivision. (It was mud now, though, because it had rained a few days earlier). In this part of the subdivision you have no need to go off-road because everything off-road comes to you. And it was to this end of the subdivision the Jeep headed— almost by itself.

My first encounter was with a packed hump of clay in the road. I usually would ease the minivan over it (on my way to ball practice). But this time I steered straight for the ridge. I revved the engine, and the front of the Jeep raised up and then rocked down. My heart began to pound. This was so cool! So cool, in fact, that when a muddy puddle came up next, I geared down, let one wheel drop in, and then revved the engine and slowly crawled out. No problem! When a truck passed me coming from the other direction, I crept up on the concrete curb—even though there was plenty of room to pass. Climbing the little curb was easy for the Jeep.

We were having fun together. I spied a broken bag of sand in the road. Muddy tire tracks curved around it, but I hit it with a vengeance, went up, and came down so hard that my glasses slid to the end of my nose. I pushed them back up, pumped the clutch, and slapped the gears like I was born knowing what to do.

As I crawled out of a second muddy pothole, I noticed some construction workers on a scaffold, laying brick on one of the new homes. They were all waving, so I gave them my very best Jeep wave. I began to think about what David had said, "Jeep people are Jeep people from the day they are born; sometimes they just don't know it."

I had some serious questions: Could I shop by night and go mudding by day? How long could I maintain this dual lifestyle? How was I going to explain this to my women's Bible study group?

After I picked up the eggs and milk, I ran the Jeep through the automatic car wash. I gave three more Jeep waves on the way home and was already looking forward to my next adventure. Maybe our subdivision wouldn't be finished for some time, and mud, sand, rocks, gravel, and potholes would be there for years to come—just like on the interstates!

"So, did everything go okay?" David asked, as I pulled into the drive.

"Just great," I said, jumping down from the high cab.

"Did it rain on you?" he asked, wiping off a few water spots with his towel.

I ignored that question and instead said, "I'm having some trouble with that Jeep wave. Is it like this?" And I did something I knew was wrong.

"No, no," David offered. "More like this." And he snapped off a pretend wave—coupled with a quick nod—with perfection. Quite impressive.

But every time I tried, I purposely looked silly.

"Don't worry about it," David said. "I mean, it's not like you're going to be driving the Jeep all the time."

Then he took (pulled) the key from my hand. Right then—in my reluctance to hand over the key—he knew. You see, a Jeep person can't hide that she is a Jeep person for long. I don't know how much time passed as we stood there like that, staring at one another by the Jeep.

"Well," I finally broke the silence, adjusting my hair and brushing some nonexistent lint from my blouse. "I guess I better take the minivan and pick up Zachary. He has ball practice later."

David took a deep breath, let it out, and then pushed the key toward me. Not until I was looking him in the eye did he speak. "Why don't *you* take the Jeep?"

I was trembling as I accepted the keys. But once I collected my thoughts I said, "Why don't *you* come with me?"

There was no need to exchange any more words. However, we did swap perfect Jeep waves. And in a few moments, we were bouncing, sloshing, and skidding—off-roading together through our subdivision.

So maybe you don't have to do *everything* together, but if you search hard enough (or sometimes just search at all) you can find *something* you can share with one another—something as simple as a handshake or a wave. Or, sometimes, it could even be something fun!

Anyway, that's how things look from up here.

Watch Out! Momma's
on the Internet

My mother used to call me on the telephone every morning around 7 A.M. No kidding, *every* morning! My brother, Mike, and I have complained about this practice ever since we moved out of her house and acquired telephones. Of course, I can't complain too much because she calls Mike first. Usually around 6 A.M.; at least I get to sleep in.

It's not so bad, really. Since the invention of answering machines and caller ID, I can pretty much head her off at the pass. And no, I just can't let it ring because then she will be in my driveway in a matter of minutes, convinced I must have fallen down the steps and now have a concussion.

This year my brother did one of the most ingenious things he's ever done: He helped my mother buy a computer and taught her how to use it. Not "real" computer stuff, mind you, but even better—he showed her how to get into those chat rooms. It's a miracle! My phone hasn't rung before eight in the morning for the first time in almost twenty years now that Mother is online. She does E-mail me fifteen times a day, but I don't mind—as long as the delete button is still working!

I wonder who thought up chat rooms? And why? Maybe someone envisioned Nobel Prize-winning scientists swapping ideas about nuclear fusion or something. But in my limited experience in the chat rooms, I have chatted (if you can call it that) with people from Alaska, New York, and Mississippi all at the same time. And do you know what we talked about? The weather.

"So what's the weather like in Alaska?" Mississippi asked.

"Kinda cold. How about you?" Alaska asked back.

Then we took turns sharing news of who had rain and who didn't and who was in the Central time zone and who was in the Pacific time zone. Big stuff like that. And that's back when chat rooms were safe, before stalkers, serial killers, and psychos hung out there. So for a long time I've always believed no good could come out of chat rooms (after all, Nobel Prize winners are too busy doing Nobel stuff to chat about the weather). Nope, no good could come of them. That is, until my mom got on the Internet.

I remember the morning she stood in my kitchen and just grinned at me.

"What, Mom? Why are you grinning?"

But she could only grin bigger. "I went into a chat room last night," she finally whispered, kicking at my vinyl floor with the toe of her shoe like a kid who's not sure if she's going to get in trouble or not.

I grabbed hold of a chair back and steadied myself. The thought of my momma in a chat room scared me and made me want to laugh at the same time. "What were you doing in a chat room?" I asked, probably coming across a bit more scolding than I should have. It's just that I had this sudden image of Momma hunkered down over her computer monitor reading, *"What are you wearing tonight?"* and then her trying to peck out, with two fingers, *"My green Kathy Lee Gifford pantsuit that I bought at Wal-Mart for 25 percent off, my purple mock turtleneck, and my flat black shoes. Why?"*

"I just made a few new friends," she said.

"What kind of friends can you make in a chat room?"

"It's a senior citizen chat room," she said, as if that were answer enough. "We just talk about senior citizen stuff."

"You mean like Social Security and Medicare and prescription drugs?"

"No, like Barbara's operation and Claire's grandson, who just got his nose pierced," she said. "Those kinds of things."

"You mean gossipy things."

She sat down, shaking her head. "No, there's no gossip going on. We're just a bunch of old people talking. Me, Claire, Barb, and Big Boy Roy."

"Big Boy Roy?"

"Yeah, that's what he calls himself. I think he's a bit bossy, though."

"Why's that?" I tried to picture Mom having a conversation with someone named Big Boy Roy.

"Well, for one," she said, "he writes in all capitals."

"And that's bad?"

She rolled her eyes like I should know this already. "Sure it is. It's just like someone screaming at you all the time. It's annoying. Barb even told him she was going to report him to the room monitor."

I laughed. This sounded so much like grade school. "Because he uses all capital letters?"

"Not only that," she added, "but last night he made everyone stop talking while he went to get another cup of coffee."

"How did he stop you?"

"He typed, 'WAIT UNTIL I COME BACK.' So we waited."

"And then what?"

"A few minutes later he came back, and we all chatted some more. Barb is in the Pacific time zone," she added.

"Mom, I don't know if this is such a good idea," I said.

She blew through her lips like it wasn't a big deal, like I used to do when I was a kid and was trying to talk her into letting me do something dangerous—like ride a motorcycle. "We're just a bunch of old folks having fun," she said. "That's all. Besides," and she started to grin again, "I can't wait to see what happens to Barb."

"What do you mean?"

"Well, last night, Barb was telling us about this house she lives in. How big it is, about her fancy kitchen and all that, when suddenly I get this IM."

"IM?"

"Instant message," Mom answered. "It just popped up on the screen, and right away I saw it was from Claire. She wanted to know if I wanted to go somewhere else and chat. So we did, and I asked her why, and she said she thought Barb was lying about her house."

"What did you say?"

"I told her she was probably right."

"That Barb was lying? How would you know that?"

"Well, if you knew Barb like we do, you'd see why we feel this way. She just goes on and on—"

"But you just met her yourself, didn't you?"

"Yes, but it's just *the way* she says things. I can just tell. Anyway, we hadn't been in this new chat room for five minutes when guess who walks in? *Barb*, wanting to know why we left her. I'm telling you, I think she has some real problems."

"What does Big Boy Roy think about Barb?"

"He can't stand her."

"How do you know?"

"Because he calls her Barbara instead of Barb."

"I see."

"Well, a few minutes after Barb pops in, in walks Big Boy Roy, shouting, I THOUGHT I'D FIND YOU GUYS IN HERE. I told him we just needed some privacy, and that's when Barb jumped on me and said that anybody who wants to can come into this chat room. Claire told her that was just fine with her, and that she and I would go somewhere else. Then Big Boy Roy told us all to STAY PUT. Just like that. Very ugly."

"So what did you do?"

"Why, we stayed put, that's what!" she said, amazed that I would even have to ask.

"So when did you talk about the grandkids and the operations and things like that?"

"That was just before the big fight."

"What big fight?"

Now Mom seemed a bit embarrassed. "Well, Big Boy Roy had to get more coffee. (You know, he drinks way too much coffee.) Anyway, I was telling Claire about my new pantsuit—you know, the one I got at Wal-Mart—so I was trying to ask her how to spell 'beige' when all of a sudden Barb goes off, typing like crazy, just because Big Boy Roy isn't there, and Claire and I are trying to have a conversation. So I type back to Barb—although I probably should have IM-ed her—"

"But your new pantsuit is green."

"I was trying to tell her it's *not* beige."

"Oh. Anyway, what did you type?"

"I just said what I used to say to you kids all the time: 'If Big Boy Roy jumped off a bridge, would you?'"

Go, Mom! I wanted to say. But I didn't think it would be appropriate to reward her for this kind of behavior. "Then what happened?"

"Then Big Boy Roy came back, and he jumped right in with his capital letters. I TOLD YOU GUYS TO WAIT, he said. And Barb starts pointing a finger at me and calling me 'instigator' and things like that."

"What did Claire do?"

"Claire kept IM-ing me. Telling me to get out of there. But I kept telling her I've got a right to this chat room, and I'm gonna stay! Then do you know what I did?"

I shook my head.

"I hit my All Caps key and told Big Boy Roy that I was going to turn both him and Barb in."

"For what?"

Mom got all flustered then. "Why, for being ugly on the Internet. There has to be a law against that. You can't go around screaming at people and bossing them around on public airwaves like that. It's just too ugly. Those chat rooms are for everybody."

"So what'd you finally do? Did you and Claire get out of there?" I had to know.

"I E-mailed the room monitor."

"You didn't."

She nodded about her bold action and grinned.

"And what did the monitor say?"

Now she frowned. "He didn't seem to care about Barb and Big Boy Roy. He just wanted to know what I was wearing. (I know I misspelled 'beige.')"

"Mom, I don't think you should be hanging out in those chat rooms anymore," I told her.

"Don't worry," she said, somewhat dejectedly. "I've been barred."

"Barred? For what?! For how long?"

"The monitor said I type too slow. I think Barb must have said something. Anyway, I can't go back in there for a couple of weeks. But I'll be back." Mom had this determined look in her eyes. (Too bad Big Boy Roy couldn't see that, I thought.)

I hadn't seen Mom take charge of her life like that for a long time. When I was a kid and she was practicing for her nurse's exam, she would draw juice from oranges with a hypodermic needle—no matter that we kids would have liked to have eaten the oranges. She did it because she wanted to be the best nurse she could be. Now I saw that same determination in her eyes.

"Oh, what time is it?" Mom asked.

"Almost noon. Why?"

"I told Claire I'd meet her at 12:30. I'd better go."

"Meet her where?" I asked. "I thought you were barred from those chat rooms."

Mom's grin was sly. "Do you really think they can keep Cyber Nanny off the screen?" And with that, she left as quickly as she had arrived—almost like one of those superheroes.

Maybe I was a bit too harsh earlier on Mother and chat rooms. It appears that some good has already come from them. Looks like Mom has learned to take care of herself. Now my greatest wish is that, one day soon, Mom will be reinstated to full chat room status. Go, Mom!

I tried to call my mother the other morning. I just wanted to make sure she was all right and that my phone was working correctly, since I hadn't heard the phone's early morning ring for so long. Mother talked just a bit, and then she rushed me off the line—she needed to sign on, she said. You know, weaning your mother away from being "all mom" is tough when you're almost forty. But weaning *yourself* away from your mommy when you're almost forty is a lot tougher.

Anyway, that's how things look from up here.

RUNNING ON EMPTY
BUT LAUGHING ANYWAY

I don't keep weapons of mass destruction in my house because, on certain occasions, I would be tempted to use them—like when I climb into the family van and find the gas gauge nailed to the empty side.

There's no doubt in my mind that putting gas in the car falls into the hunting-gathering category: find the station, gather the gas, then go to the store and get the milk and bread. Wrestling with a rubber hose is not my job, and it *never* should be my job. So when I find that gauge on dead E, I find myself rifling through the closet just to see if someone may have stored a bazooka or something in there.

I was on my way to have lunch with a magazine writer who wanted to interview me because I'm funny. At least that's what she told me. "We can meet at Amerigo's," she said, which is a nice Italian restaurant in town. "Or at McDonald's, you know, the one with the playground," and she just cackled. Being a comedian seems to bring out the comedian in everyone—ain't that a blessing.

But some days I don't feel so funny; I just feel empty. Like the day I found out the van had no gas.

Since no photographs are included with this book, let me just tell you I was wearing a cream-colored sweater (the kind that shows the slightest bit of dust) and some cream-colored slacks with perfect leg creases. My belt was black with gold trim at the tip (cinched one notch less than the week before—yes!) and shoes that hurt my feet (I forget what color they were).

I didn't notice the gas needle right away. I was just driving along, listening to choir music, waving at the neighbors as I passed. After all, going to Amerigo's always puts me in a good mood. Not even turning into the heavy traffic could dampen my spirits. I figured road rage would do nothing more than ruin my makeup.

But the moment I noticed which direction the gas gauge was pointing, things began to spin around me, much like that scene in *Twister* in which the cow flew by the couple in the truck. *I don't have time for this*, I thought. I could feel the heat rising up my neck, past my cream-colored sweater, and out my ears.

I whipped the van into a gas station and braked beside an island of cold, smelly pumps. Was the tank on this side? Or the other?

At the island next to me a clown was pumping gas into a chartreuse Chevette. *Now there's comedy*, I thought. I rolled down the window and called out to the clown, "Excuse me, sir, but can you help me find my gas tank?"

"Sure," he said. He had rainbow hair and big blue rings around his eyes. His skin was pasty white, and his gigantic nose red. He wore a loose, striped shirt and baggy pants held up with suspenders. With a little skip, he came over and began to search the driver's side of the van from bumper to bumper, checking every crevice and trim piece, pushing, and poking.

"Sometimes they hide those things," he said. He put his ear to the side and thumped the metal, then recoiled as if the gong had deafened him. He looked at me to see if he had made me laugh. Nope.

He wiped the silly grin from his face and said, "I don't see it here. Must be on the other side. Should I check?"

"No, that's okay. I'll pull to the other side. I didn't mean to interrupt you." Before I put the van into reverse, though, I said, "She's a very lucky woman—Mrs. Clown." And I pointed to the gas hose that ran from the pump into his Chevette.

Even through the greasepaint, I could tell he was blushing. He kicked at the ground with his big shoes and returned to gather more gasoline.

Switching to the other island wasn't as easy as I had thought it would be. First, I cut the wheels hard and zipped into the open lot, where two other cars had to veer wide one way or the other to miss hitting me. A couple of times someone made a move to sidle up to the pump where I was headed, but I just flashed my lights and wrestled with the steering wheel in such an intimidating fashion that finally a truck driver waved a tattooed arm at me as he blocked off incoming traffic so I could cut-and-turn my way to the right pump.

Our van has a hidden switch that opens up the gas tank. High security, I'm sure. That way no one can break into the tank and siphon off the fumes. In this same van are a lot of other switches: one opens the hood, one opens the back door, another lays the seat back in case I ever wanted to take a quick nap while jetting down the freeway. I pushed them all. Things popped open, popped loose, and popped backwards. As I squealed in frustration, I saw Mr. Clown raise his head up over the hood of his car, eyes wide. "Everything's okay," I called, waving him off. "Keep pumping!" He disappeared behind the pumps.

Even though getting gas was my number-one concern at the time, keeping my cream-colored sweater cream colored was right up there near the top. I climbed out and searched around until I found some blue paper towels on a post above a pan with a soapy squeegee. I pulled several towels out and began to stuff them, one at a time, into the neck of my sweater, like a bib. After closing all the hoods and doors, I noticed a big, black grease streak across the belly of my blue bib, just like the kind you see on those gas station mechanics who dab at the gaps between their fingers as they tell you there's something wrong—really, really wrong—with your engine.

I took down more paper towels and tucked them into my belt and folded them down the perfect creases of my cream-colored pants. Then I took a couple more and wrapped them around my hands, like mittens. I was beginning to resemble a mummy. That's when I noticed a flap on the side of the van I hadn't seen before. I crept up slowly and gazed into the opening. There it was: the gas cap.

Rightee, tightee. Leftee, loosee. (That's as mechanical as I get.) But was it *my* left? Or the *other* left, with my back to the van? And if I turn left in a circle, doesn't it wind up going right somewhere about halfway around?

I took some more paper towels, stuffed them around the gas cap, and began to turn. I got lucky, and it opened, belching out sulfur fumes that killed my appetite for Italian food—or for any food for that matter. With more paper towels, I wrestled the hose from its holder and pushed it into the tiny hole.

I squeezed the handle, but nothing happened. I turned back to the tank, pushing down my blue bib to read the instructions. "Lift . . . Pull . . . Push . . . Squeeze." This was worse than an aerobics workout (and about as smelly). I did everything. Why wasn't it working? Then the tank beeped at me. Across its face someone had taped a handwritten message that read, "Please Pay Before Pumping."

"They can trust me," I protested. "I see people pump before paying all the time. That note is just for the weirdos who look like they might drive off." I just had to get a message to the people inside. I had to let them know it was okay to let the gas flow.

I stepped away from the van and waved toward the window, my bib and mittens flapping in the breeze. "You can turn it on," I called. "Turn on the gas, please!" Over and over I called out, but no one from inside would help. I knew they could see me. Three or four of them, wearing their red service station aprons, just stood in the window and stared.

"Excuse me, miss." I turned to see the clown. He appeared to be finished pumping. Beneath his makeup, I could tell, he was a concerned clown. "Would you like for me to ask them to turn on the gas?"

"I hate to bother you to make a special trip." My bib kept drifting up into my face, and I blew it away with a puff of air.

"No problem," said the clown. "I have to go in to pay anyway."

"They let *you* pump before paying?"

He nodded, and his nose wagged. I looked down at my own costume. Boy, did I look goofy.

"Yes," I answered, "that would be kind of you." He turned and walked into the store, his feet squeaking with every step. "Hey, Mr. Clown," I called after him, "and could you please tell them I'm a comedian? I know what I'm doing out here."

He turned around and looked at me. He studied my blue paper towel outfit and thought about what I had just said, and then he broke into a big clown laugh—a laugh that probably would have hurt my feelings had I been in any other business. But I could feel the gauge inside me—the one that had been resting on empty only moments before—rising with every cackle.

It's good to make people laugh, I thought. Especially a clown.

Anyway, that's how things look from up here.

Sharing the TV on a Lazy Sunday Afternoon . . . Not!

One of my favorite things to do on Sunday afternoons is to curl up on the sofa and watch a little television. (And if I happen to doze off, that's okay, too.) The only problem is that David likes to do the same thing—but we don't like to watch the same shows.

"Oh, look, darling," he said one Sunday afternoon, browsing through the *TV Guide*. "The Masters is on. Won't this be fun?"

"You mean golf?" I asked. "On TV? Not really."

"Not just *golf*," he pooh-poohed. "The Masters!" He took my "not really" as a yes and flipped through the channels until he found the little golf show.

Now, believe it or not, I've taken up golf lately, and I'm liking it. I'll admit that maybe I like it for all the wrong reasons. I like the shiny clubs and the cute, fuzzy head covers; I like to drive the golf carts too fast, and I like the hot dogs in the clubhouse. But it's a start.

One day I might like other golf things like sand traps, divots, and shanks (whatever those are). But one thing I don't think I'll ever like—no matter how golf-crazy I might become—is watching golf on TV.

I've tried, but everything is *so* green and peaceful, and whenever people talk they whisper, so I have a hard time staying awake. But David watches it all the time, and on this particular Sunday afternoon, he had the remote control. So we cuddled up together on the sofa to watch golf.

"*That's* Tiger Woods," David said, when one of the golfers placed a ball on a tiny tee. (I like golf tees, too. One day I'm going to buy some with my name on them.) "Watch how hard he hits it," David said.

"Tiger Woods is good, right?" I asked.

Tiger whacked away. *WHOOSH!*

"Yeah, that sounded real . . . *whooshy*," I said.

"Now watch how far that thing goes," David said, ignoring me.

But it was hard to tell how far anything went. All I could see was a tiny, white ball sailing past green trees. Then it bounced a few times and rolled to a stop.

David whooped and clapped. "Wasn't that awesome?" he said.

"Which part?" I asked. "The part when it shot past the trees or the part when it landed on the ground?"

"The whole thing. It was an arc of beauty. Didn't you notice his backswing?"

My sense of modesty overtook me so I said, "I didn't pay attention to that."

Now another golfer stepped up to the ball and swung away. *SWOOSH!*

The ball sailed past the same trees and landed on the same grass and rolled to the same stop.

"Wow! Did you see that?" David cheered.

"It looked the same to me," I said.

"Oh, now watch this," David said, pointing at the green screen on the television. A golfer was hunkered over a ball, getting ready to make a putt. (My knowledge of the game was really helping me at this point.) The golfer shifted his shoulders just enough to cause the club to swing like a pendulum and strike the ball so that it rolled, ever so slowly, toward the small, round hole only a few feet away. It missed the hole, and David slapped his forehead. "Aww! How could you miss that!?" he screamed at the television.

Then the screen switched back to another little white ball sailing past more green trees and landing on more green grass. "Great shot!" David screamed. Then it switched back to another man hunkered down over another putt. This time the ball dropped into the hole. "Yes!" David leaped from the couch and shouted.

The screen then switched back to yet another white ball flying past more green trees. Before the commercial break, David was completely worn out.

Somewhere along the way, in spite of the whooping and yelping, the green screen, and the soft murmur of the man's voice narrating, the "action" lulled me to sleep. (I really believe I would rather watch someone bake a cake.)

When I woke up, David was in the kitchen making a sandwich. "How's the game going?" I called.

"Commercial's on now," he answered. "But Tiger's down by one stroke on the last hole. I'll be right in."

But before he could return with his ham sandwich, Tiger walloped one. (I'd recognize that backswing anywhere.) Through my blurry, sleepy vision I watched it sail past the trees and land in the concession stand. A vendor wearing a Coke apron and visor dove out the window and kicked over a whole tray of cups filled with Coca-Cola, sending a big, brown spray all over the gallery. I jumped up out of my seat and yelled out,

"Yes, what a shot! Wow! I've *never* seen anything like that before."

"What? What?" David said, barreling out of the kitchen with mayonnaise on his chin. He settled in front of the television. "Birdie? Eagle? Pegged it on the green? What?"

"He pegged the soda jerk," I said.

For the next few minutes we watched men in suits and dress hats ("marshals," David called them) pick up paper cups and straws and move an entire concession stand so Tiger could have room to swing. I was wide awake now. For David, the game was over. He went back to make himself another sandwich, not even caring enough to find out if the Coke vendor was okay.

Tiger's next shot landed safely in the grass, and the game slowed down again. Since David wasn't watching any longer, I surfed the channels until I found one of those cooking shows. A man named Julian was baking a cake.

"Hey, honey," I called out, "you have to see this." With all that stainless steel flashing about and flour and sugar and spoons and mixing bowls, I thought the whole scene was rather exciting.

David came bursting into the living room. "What is it? Sudden death? Did Tiger hit a miracle shot?"

"Not exactly. But this is almost as exciting. Julian is baking one of those caramel dirt cakes I was telling you about."

I waved excitedly at the television. "So *that's* how you melt the caramel. Wow, look at that!"

David turned to leave. After sixteen years of marriage, we still can't find a Sunday afternoon show we both like.

"Don't go," I said. "He's making the icing next." But David didn't seem the least bit interested so I added, "Sometimes the oven catches on fire, and they have to hose down everything with fire extinguishers."

He turned around and sat next to me on the couch. "Does that happen a lot?"

I nodded. "Sure does, especially if you have to melt anything. All that heat, you know."

So for the rest of the afternoon David curled up on the sofa with me and watched. It wasn't too long, however, before he nodded off and missed the whole part where Julian buttered the pans.

Someone once said, "Success in marriage does not come merely through finding the right mate, but through *being* the right mate." So what if David and I may never have the same taste in Sunday afternoon programming? What I saw that afternoon was that, as I napped, he was my pillow; as he napped, I was his. That's just one very small way we continue to complement each other as we work at *being* the right mate. As I watched him snooze (and drool), I liked that idea very much.

Now, if Tiger Woods would just whack a ball with his three iron right through Julian's kitchen. . . .

Anyway, that's how things look from up here.

A Fun Day Composting
with Martha Stewart

It happened again last night: I dreamed about Martha Stewart. This time she showed up wearing a denim shirt—unbuttoned, of course—over a pink T-shirt. She was standing on my back deck, waving, smiling, motioning for me to come outside. So I cinched up my terry cloth robe, slipped on my bunny slippers, and stepped cautiously out into the early morning of my dream.

I know, undoubtedly, that right now some shrink is out there writing on his scratch pad, "*Chonda seems to have an obsession with Martha Stewart, allowing her to perpetuate this ongoing struggle she has with feeling inadequate as a homemaker.*"

To that I say, "Hogwash!" Comedians have been picking on Martha for years. Just because she shows up at my house and finds me in my terry cloth robe tied together with one of David's old neckties doesn't mean a thing! Anyway, back to my dream.

"Welcome," she said, even though we were at my house. "Have you ever wondered what to do with all your yard clippings and the organic materials that come from your kitchen?"

"Not really," I answered.

"Well," she continued, ignoring me. "I'm going to show you how they can be a valuable addition to your garden as a rich food source for your plants. Follow me."

And I did, even though this was my home. We walked off the deck to the rear of my backyard where three, square, wooden bins had been constructed.

"Where did those come from?" I asked Martha. She turned sideways and traced a hand along the top edge of one of the planks. "These locally milled and planed boards have been pressure treated with a biodegradable retardant that will not harm the environment or small animals. They are perfect for creating our own compost, as we shall see today."

That answered several of my questions, especially the big one: What are you doing here?

"We'll begin with some clippings I took from your apple espalier located on your south lawn."

"I have an apple espalier? Just what is an apple espalier?" I asked.

Martha wagged a finger at me. "Yes, indeed, you have a beautiful espalier. And if you had awakened before 7 A.M., you could have seen me plant, build, and prune it for you."

"But I don't even have a south lawn," I added.

She thought for only a moment before saying, "Then maybe I built it in your neighbor's yard. At any rate," she went on, not seeming to be the least bit discouraged by this revelation, "I have some fresh clippings, and we will deposit these in bin number one." And she did, saying, "That's good. Now, bins number two and three are much older and much more advanced in their decomposition stages."

"Much older? How long have you been out here?" I asked.

"How long have you been asleep?" Martha asked with a grin. "Now, this whole endeavor is very important for the life of your plants. So if you'd like to help, we will get started. Maybe we can finish before you awaken. After all, this is your dream."

So, for the remainder of my dream, Martha Stewart and I made compost, I in my terry cloth robe, she in her Martha Stewart outfit. I borrowed her cute, plastic wheelbarrow to haul compost from my kitchen. (In real life, my organic material would have consisted of old crusty edges of pizza slices, mushy leftover Cheerios, and a few burnt corners of some blueberry Pop-Tarts. But since this was only a dream, I rolled out wheelbarrows full of leftover zucchini slices, avocado peelings, and bits of Earl Grey tea leaves.)

My neighbor came over and thanked me for her new apple espalier. "It looks just like something Martha Stewart would make," she said.

"She did."

"Then that explains it." She looked at my wheelbarrow and me and asked, "What are you doing?"

I told her, and she said she would help. She produced her own wheelbarrow, and together we began to haul mounds of coffee grounds, eggshells, and rotten vegetables from our kitchens to bin number two. We would shovel it in and then go back to our kitchens for more.

We worked hard and long, and I could imagine all my plants (and my neighbor's) thanking me for the nice meal they would receive because of our efforts. By the end of our workday, we had completely filled bin number two. As a matter of fact, it was mounded so high it spilled over the edges, feeding the grass that bordered the bin.

My neighbor and I stood, leaning on our shovel handles, and admired our work—the almost artistic mound that eggshells, peelings, and coffee grounds could make. It was heaped up higher than our heads. The breeze stirred and blew the smell of fresh compost in my face. I recalled fond memories of late nights at the Waffle House.

"Where's Martha?" my neighbor asked, interrupting my dream within a dream.

I shrugged. "Don't know. Haven't seen her for awhile." The breeze moved again, and I took a deep whiff. "Listen, I haven't had breakfast yet. Would you like to join me for some eggs and coffee?"

"Sounds good." So we parked our wheelbarrows and left for breakfast, believing the heap of compost was more than capable of decomposing without our supervision.

We ate in my kitchen that overlooked my backyard. As we ate, I noticed something rather odd about my new mountain of compost. From this angle—farther away now so I could get a better perspective, and enhanced by the mottled sunlight that filtered through the apple espalier—my compost heap looked a lot like Martha Stewart. A compost statue of Martha Stewart, if you will. At first the thought of burying Martha beneath all that compost alarmed me. But then again, like Martha had said, it was *my* dream.

Maybe my subconscious obsession with Martha Stewart is due to my house's being in such disarray recently. I don't know if this reoccurring dream is a sign that I fear I will never become a perfect, Martha-Stewart housewife, or perhaps I feel like lately I've been living in the second bin. Whatever the subliminal message my brain is sending me, I must admit, I woke up in a pretty good mood after that dream. Perhaps it was God's humorous way of putting all my failings as a housewife into perspective: Just toss them out with the compost!

Go ahead and check out books from the library about apple espaliers if you want to (if that will make you feel better). But we may never measure up to a domestic standard that someone else (who just so happens to have her own TV show, magazine, books, and columns about domestic excellence) has set for us. The best thing to do is to take a deep breath and know there are worse things than not having compost—you could *be* the compost.

Anyway, that's how things look from up here.

In Search of
the Perfect Minivan

Shopping for a new van today?" the fellow asked my husband and me as we strolled through the family section of the car lot. The guy seemed pleasant enough. Smiled a lot, too. But I'm sure he had no idea what he was getting into.

David shook the man's hand and found out his name was Russell. We had been all over town on our search, and the car salesmen always started out smiling—but we usually left them close to tears. Looking at Russell's thin smile now, I already felt sorry for him.

"Yes," David addressed Russell, "we bought a van a few years ago, and we really liked it. It was the kind that had the picnic table in the back."

"The fold-down middle seat," Russell said, nodding knowingly.

"Yes," David said, "and we're looking now to upgrade. You know, the kids are a little older now. So we're looking for something that's a bit more *family-friendly*."

"Oh, well," Russell jumped to the task immediately. "Then let me show you this new, elite model. It's just running over with fun stuff." He led us to a sleek, shiny, spaceship-looking thing that was long and skinny and looked like the front end of the monorail at Disney World.

"First of all," Russell began his spiel, "this has all-leather seats. Much more comfortable, and a whole lot easier to clean than the older cloth seats. After all, kids can be rough on a vehicle, can't they?"

"Do you have any vans with plastic seats?" I asked.

Russell just laughed and said, "That's funny. That's a good one. You must be a comedian. Now, check this out." With that he pulled on some plastic tabs that jutted out from the front dash. Out popped two cup holders.

"Only two cup holders?" David asked. "Do you have anything with more cup holders? Like maybe eight or ten?"

He giggled again. "Eight or ten? What do you need with *that* many?"

"You can never have too many cup holders," David said. "Sometimes those cups will leak, and when they do, that sugary stuff is like cement. We have a grape slushy cup that's been welded in place for about four years. So we could really use some extra cup holders."

Russell scratched his head and said, "I don't believe any of our vans have *that many* cup holders."

"And what about room dividers?" I asked.

"Room dividers?"

"Yeah," I said. "Just something simple that we could roll down from the ceiling to the floor to block off the back space into separate, sound-proof booths, something like they use at church to separate the nursery from the rest of the church." Then, as an aside, I added, "We have a teenager."

Russell nodded, seeming to understand this. "That sounds like a good idea," he agreed. "But—"

"Oh, and plenty of closet space," David added, making sure we didn't forget this feature.

"Closet space? In a van?" Now Russell was looking at us more and more doubtfully.

But I just grinned and nodded because I believed it was a brilliant idea. "Something spacious," I said, "to store extra clothes. You know, like the purple shirt my daughter will carry with her to the mall to wear just in case she gets there and her friend Emily happened to have worn *her* purple shirt after all. So my daughter will leave the pea green one stuffed under the seat, and we won't find it for several weeks—or until Emily wears her pea green shirt to the mall. I could use the extra closet space for that."

Russell hung in there with us. "Well, we could move the spare tire . . ."

"But that area might work best as a toy box," David interjected.

"A toy box?"

"Yes," I explained. "Something big enough for thousands of tiny Lego's and at least three or four Nerf guns."

Russell nodded as if he understood. "Yeah, that makes sense. Then the tire compartment could be—"

"*And* long enough for a plastic sword," David added.

"Then maybe we should measure," said Russell. But rather than measuring, he pointed out a tiny pouch that hung from the dash on the passenger side.

"That's cute," I said. "What's it for?"

"That's a trash pouch," he answered. "It'll help keep down the clutter."

I frowned as I studied the small bag, and Russell noticed. "Is something wrong?"

"I don't think that will do at all," I said. "But I know what *will* work."

"What?"

"One of those fifty-five gallon things," I said. "And I'd like one with an air-tight seal on the lid in case it flips over on the sharp turns. I'll need pick-up service twice a week. And maybe some of those blue bins for recyclables—you know, glasses and bottles. Maybe I could get a separate container for that sticky, gooey stuff that's safe to eat one day but harder than interstate pavement if left on the carpet overnight. I might need two of those."

"Anything else?"

"A vending machine," I added.

"Vending machine?"

"Yes. With gummy worms, sour cream and onion chips, Skittles, and M&Ms."

"Would you like a change machine as well?" he asked. I believe he was trying to be funny.

"Oh, no," I answered. "We can always dig around and find a quarter here and there. Unless, of course, it's stuck in the goo. But that's when the hose will come in handy."

"What hose?"

"The water hose coiled up and hanging on the side like the fire department does theirs. Then every so often we can hose down the place. *That's* why we need the plastic seats and not the leather."

"The plastic seats," Russell said, nodding as if he understood where we were coming from now.

"Yes. Just like the table and chairs at the McDonald's playland," David said, shoving his hands into his pockets and rocking back on his heels, as if our case were fully stated now. "Now *that's* the kind of van we want."

Russell just stood with his jaw dropped to his chest. (I'd seen this before—at the last car lot.) Then he gathered himself and said, "I'll see what I can come up with." He left, and we never saw him again.

"He didn't even leave us his business card," I told David.

"He's just like all the rest," David said.

"I guess there's no hope for our kind," I said, rather sadly. Then we drove away, without our dream van, on to the next car lot, where we met Phillip ...

Anyway, that's how things look from up here.

His Name Is KEN

I once made up a word: *histabore*. It's a combination of *history* and *boring*, and since you won't find it in the dictionary, I'll tell you what it means: someone who tells you his entire life story within your first five minutes of meeting him. Now, I'm not talking about people I meet while I'm out speaking. After all, I tell my life story—at the risk of boring some people—so I expect to hear theirs. But when I run into the drugstore for a can of hairspray, and I find out that the woman next to me is looking for a laxative because she ate some of her daughter-in-law's cooking—"if you can call it cooking"—and now her insides are in more turmoil than her son's floundering carpet installation business, then she is a histabore.

Things like that happen to me all the time. I used to think it was funny and just laughed about it, until the other day when I was in the corner Kwik Sak. All I wanted was some water and something salty or something sweet (I couldn't make up my mind). So I was pacing the aisle between the crackers and the chocolate, humming. That's all I was doing—humming.

"Who's that singing? Is that you singing?" came a voice from the other side of the chips.

I stopped humming, as if I'd been caught doing something illegal, and watched the end of the chip rack until around the corner walked a hairy man in a blue, greasy work uniform. The patch on his shirt said he was KEN. "Was that you singing?" he asked, pointing a greasy finger at me.

I smiled and nodded. "Just humming, actually."

"I thought that was the radio."

That sounded like a compliment to me, so I thanked him.

"I used to sing in the choir when I was younger," he said. He looked to be only about forty now. "Yeah, I had such a high voice that I was a . . . what do you call that?"

"A tenor?"

"No, higher."

"A soprano?"

"That's it. I used to have to stand in the row with the girls. That part I didn't mind," he said, shaking his head with a fond remembrance. "I could hit all those notes. But that was before I took a job with my cousin Chuck in his plumbing business."

Histabore! That's all I need right now, I thought. "That's nice," I said, feeling a little guilty at how distant and disingenuous that sounded. But I was determined to remain strong. I always gave in; I always asked more questions and wound up being late for my appointments or just missing them altogether. Not this time. This time I would not give in. I would just buy my chips and leave.

"Yeah, but I don't sing anymore," KEN continued. "Not since the operation." He was shaking his head sadly and combing through his beard with his fingers.

Operation? This was real tempting. But, then again, a good histabore knows how to pull you in, knows how to steer you down a path that winds around in a dozen different directions but never really goes anywhere. KEN was silent, staring out above the potato chip rack, just waiting for me to ask.

But instead of saying anything, I grabbed my chips (I'd made up my mind for the barbecue) and headed for the checkout stand. KEN grabbed his soda and was right behind me.

"Of course," he added, oh so slyly, "I probably should have checked the plutonium levels in the oscillating bin before the countdown ever started."

Plutonium? Countdown? I was determined to remain strong. I was next in line and would be out of there soon. But until then, all I could do was listen to KEN. I just smiled and squeezed my chips closer to me.

"You know," he continued, "you would think a Nobel Prize winner would be smart enough to check a couple of gauges and say, 'That's too much.' But then again, I've never been too good with numbers. I mean, not even a million dollars goes as far as you would think."

Nobel Prize? Million dollars? This guy was good.

"And you wouldn't believe how much trouble it is to cash in gold nuggets."

I raised my eyebrows.

"Oh, yeah," he offered at this slightest indication that I was listening. "I show one little nugget and then everyone wants to know, 'How many of these do you have?' Like I have time to sit around on my yacht and count that many gold nuggets." He rolled his eyes. "If I had time for that, don't you think I would much rather be composing another symphony?"

I almost did it; I almost asked. But the young woman at the counter was ringing up my chips and water. I handed over some money and left.

As I backed out the door, I waved good-bye to KEN. He smiled and waved back. I was rather proud of myself. From my car I watched him pay for his Coke, saying way more to the cashier than "How much do I owe you?" But the cashier seemed to have him figured out, too. She just took his money and nodded. *It's about time we all take a stand against histabores*, I thought.

On the way home I made up another word: *blockheart* (similar to *blockhead*, but much worse). That's when you hear stuff, but you block it out so it doesn't have a chance to get to your heart, which would mean that you would probably have to talk or express concern or care or exhibit some other Christlike quality. If you're a blockheart, it's so much easier to deal with a histabore. That's what that cashier was at the Kwik Sak that day—a blockheart. And that's what *I* was, too.

And that's too bad because, as I watched Ken drive away, I thought he seemed like a pretty neat guy after all—at least that's what I was thinking as I watched him drive away in his Rolls Royce, with a license plate that read NOBEL. Some beautiful music—a symphony, I think—blared out from his car, his arm moving with the count as he conducted with an invisible baton.

The cashier must have thought he was pretty neat, too. She was showing everyone the single gold nugget he had left her to pay for his soda pop.

Seems I had picked a fine day to be a blockheart.

Anyway, that's how things look from up here.

I'VE FOUND MINISTRY
IN REARRANGING
MY FURNITURE

People who are content to live the rest of their lives with their furniture in the same old places bother me. My husband is like that. Bring in a piece of furniture and just nail it to the floor.

Not me. You see, I discovered long ago that when you take the time to rearrange the furniture, things happen—and a lot of them are good things. Therefore, I move furniture. Or rather, David and I move furniture.

"Okay," I told David recently, "I want the sofa where the piano is, the piano where the table is, the table where that chair is, and the chair where that curio cabinet is."

David worked it all out in his head before saying, "And where do you want the curio cabinet?"

"I'll put that in the den," I said. "So don't worry about it until we get in there. Now, what can I do to help?"

"Just pray," he said, as he started to push the sofa away from the wall with his right shoulder. (He is so cute when he does that!)

"Do you want me to push this end?" I asked, pointing to the other end of the sofa.

"No, that's okay," David grunted. First, he pushed on the couch with his shoulder, then with his knees, then he wedged himself between the sofa and the wall and slowly unfolded like a car jack. I noticed the sofa move a bit—just a bit.

"It's working!" I called. "Are you sure there's nothing I can do to help?"

"Are you praying?"

"How about if I make us some iced tea?" I said. Moving furniture always makes me thirsty.

In the kitchen, as I boiled water and mixed in the sugar and tea, I could hear things going bump in my living room. I stirred quickly, and when I got back to where David was, things had certainly changed. Everything was now a few feet away from the walls so a furniture jam was taking place right in the center of the room, like maybe the piano had called for a huddle and the others had joined in. David was stuck in the middle, his forehead sweaty, his temples damp, and his hair plastered back to the sides of his head.

"Thirsty?" I asked.

He took the tea and drank up. "Let me double check," he said, "before I push any more. The sofa," and he laid a hand on the monster, "goes against that wall, the piano over there, the table against that wall, the chair over there, and the curio cabinet goes out of this room completely. Is that right?"

I studied for a moment. "I'd like the table there, I'm pretty sure, since that's the first thing you see when you walk in."

"Walk in where?"

"Into the room."

"It's a small room," David said. "Don't you think if someone walks into it, she'll get a good look at *all* of it in about two seconds?"

"Maybe. But I want the *first* thing that registers in her brain to be something pretty, something nice."

"How about if we park a big bass boat there? *That's* nice."

"You're already tired of this, aren't you?"

He sipped his tea and said, "Not really. I love moving furniture, and I've been looking forward to this for a long time."

I ignored his sarcasm. "Good then," I said. "Let's finish up. Now, what can I do to help?"

"Hold this," he said, handing his empty glass to me. "And keep praying."

I stepped back and watched him work, marveling at his ability to push, wiggle, walk, rock, batter, lift, and scoot everything (sometimes with an elbow, sometimes with a knee, sometimes with his head) until the traffic jam in the middle of the floor began to thin, and the furniture was fanned out in all directions. I could already tell the sofa was not going to look good against that wall.

"Oh, dear," I said, as David dabbed his forehead with a towel and rested on the piano bench.

"What?"

I stared at the sofa, hoping it would miraculously strike me as charming, but it never did. "It's just," I began, "that the sofa's a bit longer than I had thought."

"How long did you think it was?" David asked.

"I thought it would fit between the wall and the window," I said.

David looked at me unbelievingly. "Only a chair would fit between that wall and the window. Not a sofa."

"I'm sorry. How about if we swap it with the table?"

"How long do you think that table is?"

"It's shorter than the sofa, isn't it?"

"But it won't fit in that spot," he said. "Did you measure anything?"

"Then what *will* fit over there?"

David looked around the room at all the furniture he had just flip-flopped about. "The chair," he answered.

"But that chair was there before, wasn't it?"

David nodded.

"Okay then, put the chair back where it was," I conceded. "But the piano looks okay there, doesn't it?"

David shrugged. "Looks fine, I guess. But you have to kind of take a wide path so you don't whack your hip on this corner," he said, smoothing the sharp corner with one hand. "It's so big. Against that wall over there seems to be the best place for it."

"But that's where you just moved it from!"

He shrugged as if he couldn't help that.

"So what about the table? Where will that look best?"

"Well, the only place left is against that wall," and he pointed to where he had moved it from earlier.

I refused to be discouraged. "Okay. Move everything back the way it was."

"Back?"

"I'll get more tea," I called as I headed to the kitchen. "*And* I'll keep praying."

The banging, bumping, and knocking was no less than it had been the first time. I winced and moaned to think of my lovely furniture being bullied from one side of the room to the other—most of it sporting big Nike tread marks on its side. When I returned to the room, all the furniture was clogging up the middle again. But at least the sofa was turned and aimed in the direction it was supposed to go.

"Before you move that," I called out, "let me run the vacuum back there." David seemed to welcome the break and took the tea I handed him. I wriggled the vacuum into spots and crannies that were nothing more than dust graveyards. I also found $1.13 in loose change, three safety pins, and the remote control for the television that had been missing for the last two days. David cheered at this last find and spilled tea down the front of his shirt.

"So this has all been a waste of time?" David asked, as we surveyed the room. Everything was back in the same place it had been before all the heavy lifting (or heavy scooting).

"Not really," I said. "Got your remote control back, didn't you?" He grinned, and I said, "And a lot of dust died in here today. So maybe some good has been done here after all!"

Even though at the end of the day the room looked the same, it seems that every time I move my furniture a lot happens. (For one, we would still be watching C-SPAN if we hadn't found the remote.) But a woman needs to know that she can vacuum in places the furniture says you can't. She needs to know—eventually—what the piano will look like against every wall in her home. (One day I'd like to find out what it would look like upstairs, but I'll have to make more iced tea first.) And a woman needs to learn how to pray for her husband (especially when he has his shoulder against her curio cabinet).

I don't think I'll ever understand those people who *never* move their furniture. Their lives must be as stale and moldy as the space beneath their big sleeper sofas.

I think things went great that day. And in a small way, our lives were changed (not just rearranged), because a prayer went up. I can't wait to start on the den.

Anyway, that's how things look from up here.

SMOKE GETS IN YOUR EYES—AND IN YOUR HAIR AND IN YOUR CLOTHES

I wanted to take Mom out some place special for our weekly mother-daughter time together. Some place with linen napkins and two dozen types of pasta. When we walked into the place I had chosen, we were hit with the smell of tomato paste and the sounds of Italian music. (So far, so good.) An Italian-looking girl (who sounded as if she were from East Tennessee) asked, "Do you want smoking or nonsmoking?"

"Nonsmoking," Mom and I answered together.

Looking back, I don't know why the girl even asked. I don't know why she didn't just ask, "Would you rather sit on *this* side of the plastic ficus bush or *that* side?" To think that a little plastic plant is enough to separate the smokers from the nonsmokers reminds me of when I was a little girl and I believed a monster was under my bed. Shaking, I would just pull the covers up over my head. *There*, I thought, *that'll keep some big, scaly, slobbering monster with razor-sharp teeth away from me.*

Our waiter was a pleasant young man. "My name's Ed. I'll be your server." (He was blonde and looked more Norwegian than Italian.)

"This is Chonda," Mom said. "She's a Christian comedian, been on lots of Gaither videos, the Grand Ole Opry, and to New Mexico twice. I'm her mother." She grinned at Ed, who nodded at me, and said he would be back with our iced tea (sweetened, of course).

As Mom was in the midst of explaining to me all the intricacies of an operation someone in her church had had a couple of days earlier, I noticed a mushroom of gray smoke rise over the greenery and float toward us. Since Mom has asthma, I knew I had to do something quickly. That smoke was like poison. I snapped open one of the linen napkins (this was a very nice restaurant) and began to fan the cloud, which broke up into little swirls and drifted away. "Looks like we're okay for now," I told Mom. She held the other napkin over her mouth and nose and proceeded with the part of her story right after the fifteen-inch incision was made.

Ed returned with our drinks, and I pointed over the greenery. "Over there. In the smoking zone. Someone's smoking."

Ed just looked at me as if to say, "So?"

"They invaded our space," I added. "Since my mother has asthma, I was wondering . . ."

"If you can move?" Ed finished.

"Yes."

"No."

"No?"

"No. This is *my* table. And I take care of *my* people. Whatever it takes, I want you to be happy." (He must have been fresh out of waiter school.) He set down two glasses of water beside our tea, dried his hands on his apron, and said, "I'll be right back."

He disappeared for a moment and came back with two plastic pots, each filled with a small, plastic ficus tree, much taller than the little bushes that were already there. He set them up against the other plants. "There," he said, backing away and studying his handiwork. "That should help. Your *no-smoking* table should be safe now."

But already a wisp of grayish-white smoke was rising, swirling, hovering above us as if seeking us out. Ed's satisfied grin turned to dismay. "This usually works," he said, rearranging the trees and the bushes. "I don't understand." With that he plunged his head into the plastic, so deep that we could see him from only the shoulders down. After a moment he withdrew, his face as pale as the plume of smoke threatening to settle over us. "I hadn't planned on this," he announced.

"What?" I asked.

He turned to me and explained it all with a single word: "Cigar."

Mom held her napkin tighter over her mouth and began to weep. (Actually, her eyes were just watering.)

"Don't worry," Ed said, no doubt recognizing the potential for a hefty tip. "I'm a third-year engineering student at the university. I have an idea."

"Couldn't we just move?" I asked.

"No, no." Ed would have none of that. "What we need is a parabolic deflector. Quite simple to make, actually. I'll be right back." Then he disappeared, only to reappear moments later (like waiters are so good at doing), pushing a dessert cart loaded with clean dishes and bowls. He made a couple of more trips, bringing trays, bus pans, more carts, and some more plastic bushes. We watched him as he stacked dishes and lined up trays and carts so they formed a more solid wall than the shrubbery. He balanced plates and bowls with purpose, filling in the gaps with tiny dessert dishes, creating a work of such beautiful symmetry it was hard to believe he was only in his third year of engineering school.

Ed took a step back and appraised his work. "There," he said. Then he turned to us and asked, "Have you decided on your order yet?"

We placed our order, but as soon as Ed left, the smoke returned. This time it swirled through the green and yellow plastic leaves and settled like a fog around our feet. I flagged down Ed, and he screamed out as if he had seen a ghost. With his bare hands he began to fan away the smoke. Mom and I backed away slowly and watched Ed fan. We had to admire his determination.

"We can move to another table," I offered. "We don't mind at all."

"No! No time for that. Run!"

"What? Are you serious?"

"But we haven't eaten," Mom protested.

"Don't argue. Run! Run like the wind! *This wall is not going to hold!*"

"Can't we just call the manager?" I asked.

He stopped fanning long enough to twist his face into a horrific expression. "Don't you see?" he screamed. "It *is* the manager. *He's* the one smoking! Now run!"

So we left—without leaving a tip—although if anyone ever deserved one, Ed sure did. The hostess thanked us for coming, and she may have asked us to come back again sometime. But we didn't hear that part because of the loud crash—the sound of bowls and plates smashing to the floor: Ed's parabolic deflector.

I wound up taking Mom to a little out-of-the-way place where we were sure there would be no smoking. They had paper napkins, but it was a small price to pay for the clean air. A young man worked our section. He wasn't really a waiter, but he did make sure all the trays were stacked up nicely and no ketchup packets were left on the floor. And the sound of children laughing was welcomed after Ed's ear-splitting screams. Three toddlers zipped by Mom and me and dove into a big bin full of plastic, colored balls.

"Excuse me, ma'am," said the young man who was holding a handful of ketchup packets. "But if you're going to eat in there, you'll have to take off your shoes."

I slipped off my pumps and Mom slipped off her flats, and I put them in a rack already filled with lots of tiny sneakers and flip-flops and sandals. Mom took a sip of orange drink juice and asked me, "Do you think it's too late to supersize this meal?" At least we didn't have to worry about the smoke.

Anyway, that's how things look from up here.

You Know You're Nobody When the Psychic Friends Don't Know Who You Are

Have you ever tried to call the Home Shopping Network late at night and gotten the Psychic Friends Hotline by mistake? I *never* would have called them intentionally. For heaven's sake, all I wanted was a food dehydrator. The shopping network had been trying to talk me into buying one all night long. But when Darryl, the host, shoved a five-pound roast beef into this box-like contraption and in only a few minutes the whole beef had shrunk to about the size of a raisin, well, I thought that was too good to be true. So I called.

But it was late and dark and maybe I mixed up a couple of numbers, but this woman answered in a deep, breathy voice, "Hello, my name is Marie. And what is your name?"

"I'm Chonda," I answered, some of Darryl's excitement for the dehydrator still bubbling over in me.

Then Marie began to hum over the phone, low and rhythmic and kind of spooky. "I see money in your future," she said.

"A rebate? Darryl never said anything about a rebate. That's great!"

"And a mysterious dark man."

"Yeah, UPS is fine with me," I said. "Does that come with a recipe book?"

She ignored my question and hummed some more, only louder. "That situation you are worried about will become easier."

"I hope so," I said. "Trying to pack all these lunches every day takes forever. Now, I figure I can dry out a roast beef one night and serve it for a week. Like I used to do when I first got married."

After a long moment of silence, she asked, "Is there anything specific you would like to know about?"

"Yes, how much is my order?"

"Well, that depends."

"Depends on what?"

"On how much we talk."

"What does that have to do with anything?"

"That's how we charge."

"You mean, I call to place an order and you time me?"

"I wouldn't necessarily call it an order," she said. "I prefer to call it an exchange."

"An exchange?"

"Yes," she breathed. "You pay me, and I give you your future."

"This isn't the Home Shopping Network, is it?"

"No, it's the Psychic Friends Hotline."

I thought for a moment and then asked, "And how much has learning this future already cost me?"

She did some figuring and announced, "Twelve dollars and seventy-five cents."

"Twelve dollars?! Just to tell me I'm going to have money and dark strangers and my problems are going to go away?"

"Some people would pay a lot to learn those kinds of things," she said.

Okay, I thought, *I'll challenge her.*

"If you're so psychic, how come you didn't know this was a wrong number?"

"Maybe I did," she said.

"So you're a dishonest psychic?"

"Do you want to know your future or not?"

"Okay, try this," I said. "I'm going to the mall tomorrow."

"Yes."

"Will I park at Sears and go in at Dillard's, or will I park at Dillard's and go in at Sears?"

"That's not a real question."

"I struggle with the decision every time I go shopping."

"Okay, okay," she said. Then she hummed a little before saying, "You'll park at Dillard's and go in at Sears."

"That won't do," I said. "A lot of construction is going on at Dillard's so you can't park there. So I will *have* to park at Sears and go in at Dillard's. You were wrong. Can I get a refund?"

"Do you have a *real* question?"

"Okay." I rolled up my sleeves and said, "How about this: If I have to be in Dallas on Tuesday, but I'm in Ohio on Saturday, and I want the lowest fare so I'll leave on Sunday afternoon and try not to go through St. Louis but still arrive before night, can I get a room close to the airport?"

"You need a travel agent, not a psychic."

"Look, I've already spent twelve dollars. Couldn't you just squint or something and let me know about the room?"

"I can tell you about love, money, and your career, not reservations."

"Believe me, I worry about reservations a lot more than I do about love."

"I am a professional."

"Okay, one more question, and this is an easy one: How many times will Mom call me tomorrow?"

"You're not even trying."

"Maybe I just don't get it," I said. "I mean, there are plenty of things to predict about the future, if you really could predict them. Why do you need me to tell you what to predict?"

"Because you're *paying* for the call."

"I take back what I said about your being a dishonest psychic."

"Thank you."

"Why don't you tell me about something really important then?" I said.

"Like what?"

"Okay. My mom's birthday is coming up. What should I buy her?"

She didn't answer right away. I think she went into some sort of a trance or something because she started to hum again, the loudest yet. When she finally did speak, she used her breathy, husky voice and said slowly (after all, she was getting paid by the minute), "How about a food dehydrator?"

"You're good. Now why don't you hum some more and see if you can't pull out the phone number of the Home Shopping Network for me?"

I run into women all the time—Christian women—who are trying to find peace about their future. If we would all be honest for a moment, we would have to admit that some days we wish we could dial a number that would ease our minds about the future. So I found a number that helps me a whole lot when I start to feel that way.

Write it down and use it yourself: 6:31–34, from the book of Matthew. This is a good mirror verse. (Verses I print in bold letters and tape to my bathroom mirror until my brain and my heart—both—get it!)

So do not worry, saying, "What shall we eat?" or "What shall we drink?"' or "What shall we wear?"
For the pagans run after all these things, and your

heavenly Father knows that you need them. But seek first his kingdom and his righteousness, and all these things will be given to you as well. Therefore do not worry about tomorrow, for tomorrow will worry about itself. Each day has enough trouble of its own.

Sorry, Marie. I'd rather get all my peace about the future from the one who holds the blueprint in his hands—the one who said to me, "Hang up the phone and stop worrying about it."

Anyway, that's how things look from up here.

How to Relax
Without a
Time-Share Teepee

Have you ever worn yourself out trying to relax? We are a camping family, but let me tell you, after about a week of camping, I'm ready for a vacation. For that matter, after loading the van with camping gear, clothes, the dog, and the cat, I'm ready to send the family on its way and relax in my house alone!

I have a great job. I love to hear people laugh. But let's face it, sometimes life can be pretty stressful. So I go through a certain ritual to relax. I light a few candles, turn on some music, pour a cup of my favorite coffee, and sit quietly in the living room. It lasts about fifteen minutes. (Actually, seventeen minutes is my record.) Then the phone rings, the dryer stops, or Zach comes bouncing into the room. Relaxation is over.

Is it no wonder, then, that I might do a little something unusual, something not completely thought out, just for the promise of a little relaxation? For instance, have you ever received one of those letters in the mail that tells you to start packing your bags because you've won a free trip (which sort of—kind of—most likely—revolves around a time-share condominium)? The letter goes on and on about the mountains, the river, the lost treasure of Sierra Madre, and uses the word *relaxing* a zillion times. If the idea of relaxing doesn't get you all excited, the free prize they guarantee you for just taking a peek at the place causes you to pick up the phone and find a baby-sitter.

David and I once received an invitation to a resort in Kentucky. Nothing wrong with Kentucky (that happens to be where I was born), but I do think "exotic jungle" was a bit misleading. We were dirt poor, flat broke, when David showed me the letter. "Right here," he said, skipping over all the listed amenities White Clouds Resort offered and stabbing at a specific spot on the page. "It says right here that everyone participating will receive one of these three prizes—maybe even all three!" He read the prizes to me as he followed them with his finger, "A five-thousand dollar savings bond, a color TV, and/or a new car!" He held his hands up in a need-I-say-more gesture.

"I don't know . . ." I started.

"It's a win-win situation," he argued, waving the invitation at me. "*Every* prize on here is great! Besides," and he turned back to the beginning of the letter, "it says this is a pretty *relaxing* place. Come on, let's go."

White Clouds Resort was a two-hour drive from where we lived. All the way there, David talked about the prizes. "The color TV will be for the bedroom. You know how you always fall asleep in the chair during the late news. And the five thousand dollars will be Chera's college education. I'm going to see to it she can go to school anywhere she wants. And the car . . . oh, ho, ho—what color do you want?"

"Red."

"Red's good. I like red."

Then we would drive a few more miles, and he would start all over again—only I'd change my choice of car color. In his excitement, I'm not sure he even noticed.

We followed the map on the letter and came to a white frame building in the middle of a cow pasture. "Maybe it's bigger inside than it looks," David said, with hope in his voice. Once inside we found out this was just the business office. The resort was still a couple of miles away. We both felt better.

The place was packed, and the room was buzzing with dozens of conversations. Groups of three were huddled all over the room—usually a husband and wife, leaning in close as someone else talked and flipped through pictures and charts from a fat black binder. A huge bulletin board on one wall was filled with pictures of smiling couples. In just the few minutes we stood there we watched three different couples stand against a blue curtain and smile as someone snapped a Polaroid of them and added them to the large collection on the board. At the top of the board was a sign: "The White Clouds Resort Family."

A giant of a man, smoking a cigar and wearing thick, black-rimmed glasses and lugging a huge spiral notebook, came right at us. We stepped aside, but he stuck out his hand and said in a gruff voice, "Hey, I'm Jim. Welcome to White Clouds Resort. Let's find us a seat over there," and he pointed to an empty table with three chairs.

David began explaining to Jim right away that we had received this letter in the mail and—

"Do you have the letter with you?" Jim asked, his eyes appearing larger through his thick lenses.

David handed him the letter. Jim studied it for a moment and then called a woman over who took the letter. "Go ahead and match this number up with their prize," he said to her, handing her the letter. "They look like winners to me."

Then Jim winked at us with one of those I-bet-you-win-the-car winks. David squeezed my hand.

"When do you think we'll find out about the prize?" David asked.

"When we get back."

"Back from where?"

"White Clouds Resort. Come on. It's just down the road. We'll take my car." Jim grabbed his notebook and headed out the door. We followed him. His car was a station wagon—old and with lots of rattling parts. He smoked the whole time we drove deeper into the heart of the Kentucky "jungle."

"Do you guys like to camp?" Jim asked.

"Do you mean, like, *without* a bed?" I wanted to know.

"'Cause if you do," he continued, ignoring my concerns, "you're gonna love White Clouds Resort." He braked his wagon, and it came to a squeaky halt. "There it is," he said, pride swelling in his voice. (I wondered how many couples he had pinned to the board back at the office.) We were on a grassy knoll that overlooked a rolling vista of a cow pasture—with lots of teepees, nice teepees, looking like little puffs of clouds against a blue-green sky. I was wondering where the *resort* part was.

"Doesn't that look relaxing?" said Jim.

"So how many teepees do you have?" David asked, as if he really cared.

"Only twenty-four here," Jim answered, "but before long they'll be all over the country. Come on, let's take a look." Jim's wagon squeaked and rattled down the slope to the first one. It was bigger than it looked from the knoll, and instead of a slit in the side to enter, there was a wooden door. David and I stepped in. I noticed right off there was no bed, just a big, smooth, wooden floor—with a pole in the middle to hold the thing up.

Jim followed us in, and the three of us stood close in the middle to keep from bumping our heads on the canvas ceiling. Jim was grinning. "Doesn't this look relaxing?" he asked.

He drove us from one teepee to the next, and we even went inside a few more, but they all started to look alike so Jim drove us back to the office. He was excited because, he said, "I have some really great news."

On the way back, David leaned over and whispered, "What color car did you say you wanted?"

Back at the office, Jim smoked another cigar while showing us some pictures from his big black book—pictures of more teepees. David asked about things like insulation factors and the thickness of the subfloor.

"Here's the great thing," Jim said, folding his hands on the table before him to maintain his composure. "Do you know how much it will cost you to stay at White Clouds Resort for one night?" He waited for an answer so long that we both finally shook our heads. "Only *one* dollar," he answered, as he raised his hand and held up one finger. He was grinning so big now that we had to grin, too.

"And do you know how much it will cost to stay at any of the other teepees across the country?" I had visions of teepeeing in Oklahoma, or Idaho, or central Ohio. We waited for another long time before Jim raised up a single finger again and said, "Only *one* dollar."

"One dollar?" David asked.

"One dollar?" I asked.

"One dollar," he said, wagging that lone finger, " . . . and a forty-dollar-a-month membership fee."

"Forty dollars a month?"

"Forty dollars a month?"

"Forty dollars a month. But that's a small price to pay for all that relaxation, don't you think?"

But David wouldn't give in, even when someone walked by and set the Polaroid on Jim's desk, as if we were next to go up on the big board of White Clouds Resort Family Members. I was proud of David for standing his ground—protecting me and our forty dollars. All the teepee pictures in the world (or at least in Jim's big fat book) wouldn't make David change his mind.

Then the phone on Jim's desk rang, and he answered. "Are you sure? . . . How long ago? . . . Is there anything I can do? . . . Okay, you have my number." He hung up and picked up where he had left off on the cigar. He blew out a white cloud of smoke before saying, "That was the hospital. My mother's doing worse, and they don't think she's going to make it."

"Then you should go," I said, standing up to leave.

"No, no." Jim stopped us with a raised hand. "She's been ill for awhile. They'll call me if they need me. Now," and he waved a hand at the pictures of the teepees, "let's talk about White Clouds Resort."

It took David a little while longer, but he finally convinced Jim that we were broke, flat broke. "Oh, I see," Jim said, more angst clouding his face than when his mother's doctor had called earlier. "So, what did you say you did for a living? I bet we could strike up a deal that would bring your monthly membership way down. What do you think about that?" Still, David stood his ground. He was even honest enough to confess that we had just come for the prize. Slowly and reluctantly, Jim checked and double-checked our winnings before handing them over.

We didn't win the car, which was just as well because I couldn't make up my mind about the color anyway. And we didn't win the TV, either. What we did win was a certificate to *buy* a five-thousand-dollar savings bond. It was a forty-year bond that would cost us $50, not exactly free. (But when you're flat broke, that's a lot of money.)

On the two-hour drive home, David didn't talk much. And neither did our car rattle as badly as Jim's wagon, nor were we fighting cigar smoke the whole way. After what we had been through, our trip home was rather peaceful.

"Be still, and know that I am God" (Psalm 46:10a). That's what it said in the new Bible we had just won (a consolation prize). Jim had given us one of those big King James Versions with color pictures for the coffee table. (We had a choice between it or some steak knives, but I figured someone might get hurt with the steak knives.)

I guess that's why relaxing is so important to me: It's a time for me to draw closer to God. And to do that, I don't need a teepee or a discount to campgrounds all across the country. Anywhere I am, I know God is there. So if White Clouds Resort was a smoky hubbub of activity, our trip home was just the opposite; it was . . . well, a rather *relaxing* trip.

Anyway, that's how things look from up here.

MAD ABOUT
ROAD RAGE

Road rage makes me so angry. What is it about automobiles that turn even members of my Bible study into road warriors? Is it waiting in traffic?

I wait in line every day at the post office, and I've never heard anyone yell out, "How long does it take to buy a stamp for cryin' out loud?" And in the grocery store sometimes I'm backed up to the frozen food section, but never once have I heard, "Where did you learn to shop?"

I guess there's just something about being sealed up in two thousand pounds of steel that makes us feel safe to scream at someone else who's only a car's length away. But is all that rage really necessary? Why can't all the fast drivers get along with the slow drivers? Why can't all the lane changers get along with the I-was-in-this-lane-first-and-I'm-not-moving people? Why can't all the people who use their turn signals get along with the people who don't?

I figured if road rage was ever going to stop, it had to start with me—I mean, stop with me. But I sure picked a bad day to try to kick my road rage. About the same time I happened to be coming up the ramp to the interstate, an older woman with blue hair who was driving a big green Plymouth came to a complete stop in the merging lane. I was already up to forty-five, ready to gun it and zip into the flow, when I looked up and saw this green dinosaur at a standstill, the red eyes of its brake lights glowing at me. With a yank of the wheel and a quick prayer, I swerved and just missed it.

On my way past I read the old, faded bumper sticker, "God is my Co-Pilot." *Then why don't you let him drive?* I thought, but I didn't shout. I then prayed that if the next person weren't so kind, at least the blue-haired lady wouldn't get smashed.

Before long, I was in the rush-hour traffic, and the rushing was over. It was stop-and-go for the next several miles, so I applied my makeup, coifed my hair, and checked for food in my teeth.

"Hey, this ain't no beauty parlor, lady. Move it!" came a shout only a few feet away.

I turned back to see a wiry little man hanging out his window, red-faced and with mussed-up hair.

No rage, I reminded myself. *Think of something positive to say.* "You have a really strong voice," I said.

"And what's that supposed to mean?"

"Nothing, really," I said. "It's just a nice strong voice, and you should be proud of it."

He swept back his thin hair with one hand and nodded appreciatively. "I used to do a little radio in college."

"Oh, yeah? A deejay?"

He grinned.

"I bet you were great."

He blushed and laughed a little.

"Do you mind if I cut in front of you?" I asked.

He waved me over. "Yeah, go ahead. It's not like we're in a race or anything."

There, that wasn't so bad. And I had even gotten a little closer to where I was going.

About a half-mile later I needed to change lanes to make my move for the upcoming exit. I flipped on my turn signal . . . and waited and waited and waited. But no one would let me over. Now I was getting antsy. A sporty, red Mustang crept by on the right. Her window was down so I called out, "Excuse me, ma'am," to the woman with an ugly scarf around her neck.

She wouldn't look.

"Excuse me, ma'am. But could you tell me where I might find a pair of shoes to go with this outfit?" I tugged at the collar of my jacket.

"Are you for real?" she asked.

"Just desperate," I said. "I have a big meeting this afternoon, and my navy shoes look so goofy with this."

She studied my outfit. "Oh, no, navy's not it. Black, maybe. But not navy. Have you tried the Shoe Depot at Hickory Hollow Mall?"

I shook my head.

"They have everything."

The man in the car behind us blew his horn, and we both turned to frown at him.

"Here, go ahead and cut in front of me," she offered.

"Oh, I couldn't do that."

"Please." She waved a hand to the gap before her.

"Thank you so much. That's a really nice scarf you're wearing."

She grinned, and I changed lanes.

I believed I was onto something here. People like kindness; they like smiles; they like compliments. Just treat people like you want to be treated—that's always the secret in those "secret to success" books. And with this new face of kindness I was developing, I could possibly even—

Just then the big green Plymouth I'd nearly smashed into earlier zipped past me, cutting me off so sharply that I missed my exit and I was back in creeping traffic and would be for at least the next three miles. My heart began to pound, and my blood began to pump (especially into my face). I squeezed the steering wheel so hard my hands hurt.

For a long way I had to ride close on the Plymouth's bumper. "God is my Co-Pilot" seemed to mock me. When I finally had a chance to move up beside her, I got ready to give her one of my special mean faces, the kind I make when I'm putting lipstick on my bottom lip—mean and huffy. If anyone deserved a shot of road rage, she did. But before I could do or say anything, she met me with the sweetest, biggest smile. I couldn't say anything. Her face just seemed to glow (making her hair that much bluer).

That's the kind of smile I had been trying for earlier. But you just can't fake that kind of smile. The old woman pulled down on her turn signal, and I couldn't help but point the way in front of me. As she switched over, I'm sure I saw her talking to someone in the passenger seat, although it seemed pretty empty to me.

Then I knew I had been only partly right earlier. I can smile and be kind, but I also have to be genuine. If not, all I have are some hollow lane changes during rush hour.

By being genuine, maybe I'd even affect someone's day like that little old woman did mine. All day long I thought of her. Not about how she can't merge and nearly killed me and several others on the merging ramp, not about how I had to go to the next town to turn around and then had to apologize for being a half-hour late for my meeting, and not about how she had the bluest hair of anyone I'd ever seen (over eighteen, anyway). Instead, her smile stuck in my mind, a smile that said, I love you, even if you don't let me cut in front of you. Wow!

That's what I'm going to practice today on the way home, and tomorrow on the way into town. Road love. Because, after all, God is my co-pilot, too.

Anyway, that's how things look from up here.

WHAT PART OF "TEN ITEMS OR LESS" DON'T YOU UNDERSTAND?

The young woman's hand seemed to move in slow motion. All I could do was stand frozen and watch as she reached higher and higher, until her fingers twisted around a cotton string that was attached to a beaded chain that was attached to a light switch. With a quick yank on the string, the plastic number three began to blink. Then, still in slow motion, she lifted a black phone from its cradle and spoke into its mouthpiece. Her tired voice rang throughout the store, "Price check on aisle three, please. Price check on aisle three." It looked like another long day at Stal-Mart.

And I was next in line, too! I thought I had picked a good line. The woman in front of me had only two items—but one of those turned out to be a turtleneck sweater with no price tag. After the cashier made her announcement, she stepped away from the register, folded her arms, and leaned against the wall of her little cubicle, getting comfortable. Now, this was not the first price check I'd lived through—housewares, electronics, kids' wear, I'd had lots of experience. But women's wear was big trouble.

I know women who will pick up a blouse and fall in love with it. But, as the day goes on, usually somewhere in the automotive section, the love affair ends, and the blouse is left hanging from a spark-plug display. "It's okay," the woman says. "It gives the workers something to do." And I'm convinced that part of the workers' job is to remove the price tag before they find its home.

By the time that blouse can be matched up with like blouses that do have a price tag, I was thinking, *my ice cream will be melted, my cabbage wilted.* Yes, I should have known that a turtleneck sweater was trouble.

I gritted my teeth, gripped the buggy handle, and pulled back from aisle three. For a moment I just hovered in the No Buy Zone—you know, that big area in front of the registers where you don't shop, but you cruise back and forth in search of the perfect checkout line. I noticed the light for aisle seven was on, so I set out. My wheels squawking, I yanked the cart a hard right rather than try to roll the long way around the popcorn display. (Someone always puts up the oddest displays in the No Buy Zone. Cheaper than speed bumps, I guess.)

Aisle seven would take you even if your cart was crammed full and overflowing—or even pulling a second cart in tow, like the train that cut me off. The train's driver saw me coming, I know she did, and if it hadn't been for the box of Cap'n Crunch that came flying out of the second cart, I'd have beat her to the belt. But I had to brake hard to avoid the cereal box, which allowed her carts to zip in before mine. The mother pushed and tugged her buggies into the channel. With a hard look, I studied the toddler in the second cart as it passed by me. He was grinning, mouth smeared with something sweet. He waved at me and pointed at the Cap'n Crunch. I smelled a conspiracy.

No time to lament. I spun the cart 360 degrees (barely missing the Titanic bath soaps display).

Number three was still flashing, the cashier still resting. But now light one was on—and the lane was empty! I pushed the cart hard and felt my cargo shift. On the way past three, I noticed the woman who wanted the turtleneck was pulling and tugging at the sweater, searching inside the neck, under the arms, everywhere for that elusive price tag.

I slowed and came into aisle one at a safe speed. There to greet me was a young girl with lavender eye shadow, green lipstick, and black fingernail polish. (I am not making this up.) In between the chomping sounds she made on her wad of bubble gum (bigger than my fist), she was talking to the cashier at the register next to her about Billy Earl and something about a fistfight with Ernestine and how "Mamma's done kilt 'em both." (I'll interpret for you later.) In the middle of her sentence, she glanced my way for a split second, long enough to say, "Sorry, ma'am, but this is the express lane. Five items or less." I kept waiting for her say, "Just kidding" or "Come on in. I'll take you anyway," but she didn't.

Rather than move, I studied my load. I didn't have too much. "I think I'm close on the count here," I told her, ashamed at how pleading my voice sounded.

Just about the time Billy Earl had done went down to Tucson and bought a double-wide, she put one hand on her hip and finally looked at me. "Maybe you are close," she said. "But sometimes we have customers who have small emergencies, like sick children at home, or they've run out of diapers, or they need batteries for their flashlights because the power has been knocked out. Things like that. That's what this aisle here is for, so people with real emergencies don't have to wait so long."

I looked back. There was no one behind me. "There are no emergencies right now!"

She chose not to hear this and instead said, "Perhaps you should try . . ." she paused as she scanned across the aisles, " . . . aisle three. It looks like she can take you over there." And she went back to planning her outfit for whenever Billy Earl got back from Tucson.

I looked over to aisle three and saw that the light was on and not flashing. "You're serious?" I asked. I studied the hostess of aisle one, but all she did was shrug her pretty little shoulders and say, "Store policy."

I jerked the buggy backwards, the wheels grinding and bouncing and leaving a dotted black skid mark on the tile floor that someone would later probably have to use a giant buffer to remove.

The cashier at aisle three saw me coming; I know she did. And I saw her leaning back against her little cubicle, arms folded, yawning. I clipped a tin of popcorn on the way past and sent it wobbling into the path of an oncoming buggy. I thought about the little toddler in buggy number two, tossing out boxes of Cap'n Crunch that worked like mortar shells to keep incoming buggies away, and felt rather proud of this tactic. But before I arrived at the conveyor belt, before I could grab up that little baton and slap it down on the black surface to keep someone else's groceries from getting mixed up with mine, the yawning cashier picked up a cone-shaped object that advertised cigarettes and set it down on the belt. Below the advertisement was the note, "This Register Closed."

"You mean *after* me, right?" I said.

"Sorry, but it's my break time." She yawned, slipped out of her cubicle, and walked away.

"Aisle seventeen is open with no waiting," blared a voice over the PA system. Again, I reversed out of the aisle and turned my buggy in the direction of aisle seventeen, which was so far away. I doubted my own strength and stamina to make it that far, just past the flea and tick display, well beyond the cage of big rubber balls. Frozen in place, I couldn't move. In moments, my heart slowly sank as I watched a tiny buggy (at least it looked tiny from that far away) slip into the spot marked aisle seventeen. I could only lean forward on my buggy, parked motionless beside a cardboard cutout of the Titanic, and watch my hope slip away. But I wasn't going to cry.

I knew then that I had no other option. I began to throw items overboard: Pringles, plastic coat hangers, shoe polish, some fuzzy socks with rubber grips on the bottoms, and at least a half-dozen other odds-and-ends, until I was down to five items. (The socks dangled dangerously from the bow of the Titanic, but that would give the workers something to do.) Then, with renewed determination, I turned my buggy about and aimed again for aisle number one, the express lane.

"Hi, remember me? Just wanting to hear if Billy Earl got the double-wide back to Tennessee." (Okay, I'll admit I said it with a bit of sarcasm. She was not amused.) Before she could say anything, I told her, "I have five items, and I'm in a hurry—this is an *emergency*."

She smiled because that was what she was supposed to do. "Did you find everything you needed today?" she asked, as she began to scan my items.

I had kept a pair of big fuzzy house shoes, and she picked them up and studied them as if they were a puppy. "How cute!" she squealed. She turned them over once, twice, without finding what she was looking for. When she reached for the cotton string that dangled just above her head, the string that was attached to the chain that was attached to the flashing light, I grabbed the shoes from her and laid them on the chewing gum rack beside the register.

"I'll get those some other time," I said.

She looked confused. "But they're *so* cute!"

I took my four items and left, wadding up my shopping list and stuffing it in my pocket as I walked. Before I could get to the door, I heard a voice on the PA. I recognized it as the sleepy voice of the cashier on aisle three. She was asking for a price check from women's wear on a pair of fuzzy socks with rubber grips on the bottoms.

Later that evening, my husband called to tell me he was on his way home. "Can I pick up anything for you on my way?"

I pulled the crumpled shopping list from my pocket and flattened it out on the counter. "As a matter of fact," I said, "while you're out ..."

Anyway, that's how things look from up here.

A REAL CLEARANCE ON SCENTED SUITS

The other day I read a story about a new suit for men—a scented suit, as a matter of fact. I'm not kidding. They make them in South Korea, and these suits sell for about $400. (Do you know how many pine-tree air fresheners you can buy for that?)

The secret to the suit, I read, is in these microscopic capsules implanted in the fabric. When the fabric is rubbed or shaken, the capsules pop open to release the scent of lavender, peppermint, or pine. Okay, stop laughing; this is a true story!

I can see where something like this could come in handy. Every time David and I get lost and I make David go into one of those convenience stores to ask for directions, he comes back smelling like Marlboro country. But if he had on one of those lavender-scented suits, he could just do a little two-step in the parking lot and come back into the car smelling like a butterfly bush. That's when one of those suits would be nice.

But I can think of a few instances in which smelling like a pine tree could be the worst thing. Think of how dangerous it could be to your health to come across a bear while walking through the Smokies in a pine-scented suit on your way home from church.

And I wouldn't want to wear one of the lavender-smelling ensembles, either. Think of all the bees you'd attract during the spring months of cross-pollination!

But what if not only scented suits caught on in a big way but also scented clothing of all kinds? Why stop with peppermint, lavender, and pine? Why not take the scented thing as far as it will go? It only makes sense to me.

If you ask most people what two things they like the most, they would probably say food and clothes. So why hasn't someone thought of this before? Children's clothing could be the fun smells of jellybeans, bubble gum, and tutti-frutti ice cream. Adults could wear grown-up smells like fried chicken, okra, and squash (or just meat and potatoes for people like my husband).

Food-scented clothing could help boost sales for some small businesses. For instance, if you sell pizzas and you want to drum up a little extra business, just jump into your pizza-scented coveralls, grab some business cards, and head out to the mall. And waiters could actually wear the soup of the day so, when you ask them what it is, they don't just stand there going, "Ahh ... ahh ... I'm not sure, but I'll find out." They could just sniff their shirtsleeves and know.

Food-scented clothing could help one's self-esteem. I love the smell of popcorn, but I hate the way my feet smell after being hot and sweaty in my sneakers all day. But what if I had popcorn-scented socks? Then, at the end of the day, my feet would smell just like a bowl of Orville Redenbacher's extra buttery. (Everyone would love me!) And what could be more relaxing than, after wearing my roast beef with gravy pantsuit all day, to come home and slip into my chocolate brownie pajamas?

Dressing for the seasons would be more fun than simply "flannel in the winter and rayon in the summer." On the coldest days, I'd love to wear my chili con carne sweatshirt with my saltine mittens. And on really hot days, I'd wear something fruity, like watermelon or kiwi.

And think of the time food-scented clothing would save, too. Instead of standing in front of the closet every morning and spending all that time trying to match up colors, I could simply match smells (and plan for supper at the same time).

I know there would be some problems. "You can't wear fish with pasta," someone would say. But look at not only all the different choices that would be available to you but also the combinations. Of course, my husband would be happy to knock around in the ground beef sweatshirt and pants with cheese socks, pickle T-shirt, and a ketchup ball cap, smelling like a cheeseburger all day. Me? I'd love to take a gourmet clothing lesson or two and be a different casserole every day—perhaps even a quiche every now and then.

I don't doubt that clothes would still be a marker of status. It would be obvious (without labels) who was wearing the filet mignon skirt and jacket and who was wearing the cheap sirloin skirt and jacket. There would be those who would insist on wearing a caviar camisole or perhaps an escargot dinner jacket just because they thought they should.

I don't doubt, either, that some fake stuff would be going on, causing us all to be more aware of the scams, to be on watch for imitation crab meat sweaters, powdered milk blouses, ground turkey slacks, things like that. We would have to be on guard constantly and schooled regularly to distinguish the genuine from the pretend. (Imagine your embarrassment at attending a formal function wearing what you thought was a genuine lamb chop sequin gown only to discover it was some soybean byproduct.)

Meeting people would be more than just shaking hands and asking about jobs. "Oh, I just love the smell of that outfit!

What is it? Egg roll? Without MSG, right?" But the downside of this is that complete strangers would stop you to sniff your clothes. "Sorry. I thought I detected the aroma of cabbage stew."

And I can imagine the conversations I would have. "Chonda," my friend would call to say, "what are you wearing tonight?"

"Since we're just going out to the mall, I figured I'd wear my black olive slacks and that pimento blouse that I showed you the other day."

"Oh, shoot, I was going to where my pimento top, too, but don't you think that will be too much pimento?"

"Not at all. David's wearing this nifty egg salad sweater that I got him for Christmas so we should be okay. We'll just make sure he stands between us. What about your husband?"

"Well, he has this pickle thing he could wear."

"Any mayonnaise or cream cheese?"

"Just in dress slacks, but I think he wanted to go a bit more casual. How about mustard boxers?"

"Perfect."

Food-scented clothing may be the best idea since the Y2K-scare books. (I wish I had invested in those.) They will encourage us to love our neighbor more. (I've stood in line next to people I could have loved a whole lot more if they had just smelled like a Salisbury steak.) And I believe food-scented clothing will also help people to lose weight. I mean, if you walk around all day smelling of meatloaf, the last thing you're going to want to dig into is a fatty meatloaf recipe that night. (If your weakness is bratwurst, the same thing holds true.)

Going to the mall would be like going to Luby's Cafeteria. Going to Luby's Cafeteria would be like going to Sak's Fifth Avenue. Food and clothes, clothes and food, together at last. Life would be good!

But I was just wondering: Would I need more closet space or a bigger refrigerator?

Anyway, that's how things look from up here.

BORN TO SHOP:
IT'S A GIFT

I'm writing this chapter as a warning to women everywhere who love to shop, who love to meander through the malls, moving from one sales rack to the next. If this is you, then you know you are either born with the love of shopping or you aren't. This love that I'm talking about—the thrill, the reckless abandon—can't be faked. Nor can it be forced upon a spouse who doesn't possess it. This is where my warning fits in. If the desire of one party to shop is not genuine, then you need to be prepared for certain dangers. The side effects can range from simple discomforts, such as fatigue (watch for repeated yawning—even at a 60 percent-off rack), or something more serious, such as a blurred sense of reality (evidenced by an inability to understand the difference between horizontal and vertical stripes). You see, I know this firsthand because I tried this with my husband, and I'm not proud of it. This is my story.

It was all my idea. I'd seen David use his skills in the hardware store: zipping from the paint to the electrical and then back to the plumbing, loaded to the hilt with supplies and never once using a buggy. Because of this, I believed I could make a mall shopper out of him.

I wanted to make this transition easy for him. I even took him to a mall with the simplest floor plan: an upstairs and downstairs with north, south, east, and west wings. Nothing too complicated. A Victoria's Secret was located on each level to sort of break up the clothing and shoe stores that all look alike to men.

Right away I made a purchase, one of those quick kinds where you see it and you just know you have to have it. I believed a quick purchase like this would get David's adrenaline pumping. But, like I said, you just can't force the *thrill*. I had fallen in love with a pair of slacks, dark blue with double pleats in the front. "They'll go with practically *anything*," I told David. He just nodded and appeared to make a mental note.

"That was quick," he said, taking the shopping bag for me and grinning. "This wasn't bad at all. I'll get the van, and you can wait here."

"Oh, but we're not finished," I said, and his sweet smile broke up into tiny pieces that fell away until nothing was left of it. *He's going to have to toughen up if he's going to run with me*, I thought. "Follow me," I added, and took off at a pretty quick pace, having just spotted a big, red "Clearance Sale" sign way at the other end of the mall.

"These are so nice," I sang about the clothes on the circular rack. I slowly worked my way clockwise around the rack.

David stood to the side and watched. "Why do you touch every piece?" he asked.

Here was my chance to teach him. I've always known that education leads to appreciation (ever since I read it on a bumper sticker). "This is the touch test," I explained. "When I do this, I get an idea of the material's quality, its weight, and its thread count."

"Thread count?" Now he seemed interested.

"Of course," I said, continuing my way around the rack. "The greater the thread count, the more durable the fabric. You know, like one hundred, two hundred, three hundred. The greater the better and, therefore, the longer the piece will last. That way you can sort of gauge if you're getting a good buy or not."

I'm pretty sure he brightened up. A salesclerk walked past, and David flagged her down. "Excuse me, ma'am. Can you guide us to your merchandise with the best thread count? Perhaps a three hundred or four hundred. A thousand, if you have it. Maybe even higher."

"I'm not exactly sure where that would be," she answered.

"They don't group clothes by thread count," I explained to David, and the clerk left.

"Why not?" he asked. "It seems like that would sure save you time. Suppose you needed a blue shirt—okay, blouse— with a three hundred thread count right away for some big function. Well, if they kept all the three hundred thread count shirts in one place, then you could zip in, zip out, and still have time to do other things—like eat hors d'oeuvres and things like that."

I could tell his experiences in the hardware store had just about ruined his potential as a serious mall shopper. I finished browsing through the first rack and started on the next. "It just doesn't work that way," I tried to explain. "Sometimes a *lighter* fabric is better." I pulled out an orange blouse with a dark blue flower print and held it up in front of me. "How does this look?" I asked.

David studied it for a moment and then said, "Like patio furniture."

I shrugged and put it back. He was partly right. As he walked past, he reached out and rubbed the orange shirt. "Besides, it doesn't feel like a very good thread count."

Our next stop was Dillard's, but before we got there, I spied a long chartreuse jacket that caused me to swerve into a small shop. I picked the jacket from the rack and turned to David and said, "Now I just *love* this."

David's eyes were wide with admiration as well, and I was beginning to believe we had just connected, when he said, "Yeah! I caught a lot of bass on a worm that color!" He rubbed the material as I plunked it back onto the rack and headed for the next store. "Feels like a great thread count, too," he called from behind me.

In Dillard's, I moved to the sales rack, and David followed. "Look at these," I said, raking a hand along a batch of jackets and blouses before I would move through them one at a time. "And they're 60 percent off!" David can grasp numbers better than he can grasp color schemes.

"Sixty percent off what?" he asked.

"Off . . . what it usually costs," I answered.

"Oh, then that must be pretty good."

"It's excellent!"

Another clerk walked past, and David flagged her down. "Excuse me, ma'am, but these clothes are on sale, right?"

"Oh, yes," she said. "They're 60 percent off."

"Off what?"

"Off . . . what they *used* to be."

David looked suspiciously at me. "You guys have some sort of a code, don't you?"

"We have more to choose from on the other side of that wall," the clerk added, pointing across the room. She was so helpful.

Then something happened that makes a true shopper giggle. (Only because it would attract too much attention to shout for joy.) I found something I really liked, *and* it was on the 60 percent-off rack. It was a red suit with black piping along the collar and gold brocades on the cuffs. "I'll bet this really looks good *on*," I said to David.

"You don't think it looks good now?" he asked. "Right there on the rack? Then why would you even consider it?"

"Of course I think it looks good. But it's hard to tell about the shoulders and how the tucks will fall along the waistline. Here," I said, handing him my purse, "I'm going to try this on." So I left David standing there with my purse, in the middle of the day, in the middle of the women's department in Dillard's.

I tried on the suit and stepped out to check myself in the mirror. David came up from behind, clutching my purse as if it were a dirty diaper, and said, "It looks the same to me as it did on the rack."

"Oh, no, see how the shoulder pads stand out? Notice the little tucks on the sides?" I wiggled the jacket. "I really like this." Which was my way of saying, "I want to buy this."

"Well," David said, clutching my purse up under his arm, a more comfortable position, "then this must be our lucky day since they just marked it down to 60 percent." (I was getting more hopeful that David would make it as a mall shopper.)

For the rest of the day we shopped. (I caught David yawning several times but ignored the signals.) I bought things, and David carried the bags. We ate at the food court. And for his sake, I made two out-of-the-way trips past Victoria's Secret. I was about to wrap things up—I was simply going to look on the way out for a pair of rust-colored shoes with brass buckles (I promise that was all)—when things began to unravel.

"Now *I* really like that," David said, his voice sounding so tired. He was pointing at a lavender dress with horizontal stripes. The sleeves were too lacy, and the neckline way too low. But with an effort, David walked into the store and pulled the dress from its rack (clearly marked 45 percent off). "See," David said, holding up the dress so that it covered him. "It's on sale," he said. "And feel this." He pushed the dress toward me. "If that's not a good thread count, I don't know what is. And, you

know, lavender will go with just about anything." He was serious. (And he was losing it.)

"But these are *horizontal* stripes," I pointed out.

"So?"

"So horizontal stripes make me look fat," I explained.
"Horizontal stripes make everyone look fat. Vertical stripes are
what we want."

"Well, why don't you just try it *on*?" he said, offering me
the dress. "Maybe it looks better *on*. Did you ever think of that?"

That's when I realized he had been in the mall way too
long, that I had pushed him way too hard. "That's okay, honey,"
I said, pushing him and the dress back toward the rack from
which it came. "How about if we buy an ice cream cone at the
Dairy Queen and head back home?"

"So would you rather search for some vertical stripes?" he
asked. "Because if you do, I'll help you find some vertical
stripes."

"No, no," I said. "Let's just get some ice cream."

"They'll make you look skinny."

I pushed him in the direction of the rack. He reluctantly
put back the dress and followed me to the ice cream shop.

"Did you have a good day?" I asked him.

He nodded and said, "I'm sorry we couldn't look for the
rust-colored shoes with the brass buckles like you wanted."

"That's okay, really," I said, taking him by the arm.
"Maybe next time."

"Hey, next time, do you think we might rent one of those
strollers like you push babies around in, only we can pile it up
with shopping bags like the other mommies?"

"Of course," I told him. "We can even rent one built for
twins."

"That would be great."

"I'll take my purse back now."

"Sure."

I guess it's true what they say: Men just aren't wired the same as women. And it's best if we don't try to rewire them.

I guess my day could have been worse, though. He could have bought the lavender dress with horizontal stripes and worn it home—or even worse, given it to me!

Anyway, that's how things look from up here.

BITTEN BY THE
SWEEPSTAKES BUG

I used to get all excited when I received one of those fat envelopes in the mail with my name stamped all over it. When I see my name stamped on anything I get excited. After all, when your name's Chonda, you can't ever hope to find a coffee mug or pencil with your name on it. And without even opening the envelope with my name stamped in large letters, I could see I was really close to winning $11 million.

I used to work hard on all the stuff that came inside the envelope, too. I'd fill out the forms, choose the color car I wanted, and write legibly on the blank check exactly how I wanted *my* check to be made out. But for all the work, a few weeks later I'd only receive another fat envelope in the mail that said, "CONGRATULATIONS, *CHONDA*! YOU HAVE MOVED INTO THE FINAL STAGES OF WINNING OUR $11 MILLION GRAND PRIZE!" It seemed every step I took only moved me into the finals—but never into being a winner.

So I don't get excited about that mail anymore. As a matter of fact, I get more than a bit perturbed—especially since I discovered that everybody else I know, even the ones who throw away the envelopes without even bothering to open them, have also reached the final round.

I started to toss the latest notice into the trash can, but then I remembered reading a long time ago about an old man who entered all sorts of contests and won, simply because he would put the stamps on upside down and sign his name with a crayon. (I guess he got some sort of sympathy vote.) At any rate, this old man's story started me thinking that maybe there is something to being a little "sorry." Maybe that could be the one thing that separated me from the other two finalists on the list.

So I decided to try it. I stuck all the stickers on upside down (with that thick, milky glue that gets all over everything). On the pieces I was supposed to tear off and send back, I cut in a zigzag line (as if I'd been taking cough medicine only half an hour before operating the scissors). I used an envelope I had received from the phone company, scratching out its name and putting the sweepstakes address on the front. When I stuck the envelope in the mailbox, I remember thinking, *That has to be the sorriest entry in the history of sweepstakes. It deserves $11 million.*

If the glue and the envelope didn't get them, I figured the letter I had enclosed would:

Deer sweepstakes winner picker,

I'm excited about sending off for your sweepstakes. I'm sorry I haven't sint anithang sooner, but I had to feed all my babies (3 of 'em!) an wait for my oldest boy to come home from kender—kin—kinnergar—from skool. (He has the only box of crayons in this famly.)

That red car looks good to me. (I love the color red.) An my babies like it too. Did I tell you I got 5 youngins? But they good kids. They ain't never once asked for no $11 million. Anyways, i cut out a picture of that red car and glued it to the page like you said. It looks *a bit crooked to me, but since I'd been chasing chikens all mornin I wusn't sure if it wus me or my gluin.*

I wouldn't had to chase no chikens, though, had my huzbend fixt that fince. But he says them boards is expin—exspins—cost too much. I just want to by some bords to keep my babies safe (all 8 of 'em) and to keep the chikens in—so my famly can eat, you know. (I don't even know how much $11 million dollars is. Is that enough to buy bords to fix my fince?)

Corse that fince would a never been broken if it hadn't a bin for the earthquake. Oh, yeah, didn't I tell you? The ground jus shook an opened up and swallowed my babies—all 11 of them—all of 'em (except for the one in kindter—kinner—in skool).

And when that boy come home, I sent him back into town with our old cow and told him to swap it for some food. But he came back with a handful of beans—magic beans, he says and—oh, sorry, I must have been thinkin bout last week. This week I made him and his daddy chop down a tree and build me a ladder. Then I clumbed right down into the belly of that dark earth and pulled out all 16 of my babies. We wus so happy that we danced around (all 18 of my youngins) and broke the fence.

Anyway, I noticed in your sweet letter to me (with all them sticky pictures and fill in the blank things) that $11 million could be allocated either in smaller doses over a longer period of time (in accordance with the various local and federal tax statutes, of course) or in larger doses assigned to my choice of either mutual funds or tax-deferred annuities. For your records, I would prefer the annuities (and definitely not the high-yield, interest-bearing bonds), or if your people would be so kind as to contact my broker at 555–1842 and allow him to discuss, with my people, an aggressive stock and bond campaign, which he has so diligently tailored to fit my needs, then that would be much appreciated.

So I guess I better go now and start supper. It takes a while to get enough grub for 21 youngins, you know. And besides, these is the only crayons we have, and my oldest will be in from kinter—kinnyg—

kiter—from skool real soon. Thank you and come eat with us sometime if you're in the neighborhood. You might have to catch your own chickin though.

Signed: Someone who jus wants to git her fince fixt (and feed her 27 babies).

So that's the letter I sent. At first I was afraid I might have overdone it on the fence thing. After all, I did mention it three different times. (I do wish I'd said more about the children—all 31 of them.)

But my fears proved to be unfounded because in only a few weeks I received another envelope from the same company. I was in the top three—and the company wasn't sure if they would be able to locate the other two in time for the drawing! Things were lookin' good for me an' the youngins.

This world seems full of empty promises, which lead to so many disappointments. The more I heap my hope on things as shallow as an envelope with bold, black ink pronouncing me only a postage stamp away from riches, the more disappointed I become. By the way, apparently they found the other two contestants, because no one ever showed up at my house with a little red sports car, and my stockbroker only called to ask if I was *ever* going to do any business with him.

That fat envelope, which seems to come every month, doesn't hold the promise that will feed you or your children (even if you do have 31 youngins!). That promise is found only in something a bit meatier than stickers and cut-out coupons: the Bible and the simple image of the cross. Just open it up and read the words for yourself—especially the red ones.

Anyway, that's how things look from up here.

I Can't See the Clutter for All the Stuff in the Way

Here's something that bugs me so much I've had to type this sentence over five times because I'm so worked up I keep hitting the wrong key: *clutter.* I can't stand it. I don't understand where it comes from, and I'm not really sure what to do with it once I find it.

David does. "Toss it out!" Of course, that's what he says about anything that can't be used to catch a fish.

Just the other day I was trying to make my way from the upstairs bedroom to the kitchen for a nice, relaxing cup of coffee, when I tripped over an old wicker basket in the bedroom. I knelt to study the workmanship and the frilly ribbon and bow that adorned its handle (and to make sure my toe wasn't broken).

"Are you okay?" David asked, having heard me cry out.

"I'll be okay."

He poked his head in the door and saw me kneeling by the basket, rubbing my toe. He shook his head and walked out. "Toss it out!" he called back.

"But it's so cute," I said. "It's the welcome basket from when we moved into this house."

"That was two years ago," David said, finding it easy to dismiss anything of sentimental value. "You can't keep that thing forever. Toss it out!"

I rubbed the pain away in my toe and set the basket on the dresser, next to a box of wrapping bows we had saved from the presents this past Christmas (three months ago, now). David was supposed to have put those in the attic along with the Mexican blankets we had brought back from our anniversary trip last summer. They were five bucks apiece, so I bought a half dozen. I just hadn't had time to pass them all out yet. *If David would just put them in the attic,* I reasoned to myself, *they wouldn't be in the way at all.*

I limped on down the hallway and had to turn sideways to get past the old rocker that used to be in the living room. We had moved it into the hallway to make room in the living room for the curio cabinet I bought to display my little China doll that used to belong to Minnie Pearl.

"Isn't there a better place for this rocker?" I asked, hoping David would hear me.

"Toss it out!" he called out.

"I think the garage would be a better place for it than in the middle of the hallway," I said.

"The garage is full."

"And what is *this* doing here?" I said, pointing to my daughter's electric guitar and amplifier that were blocking the hallway as well.

I looked at Chera accusingly when she popped her head out her bedroom door. She defended herself by saying, "There's not enough room in my room. Maybe if Dad could put my old Barbie doll collection up in the attic . . ."

"The attic's full," came David's voice, like the Wizard of Oz from the other side of the curtain. "Toss it out!"

"We can't throw out *everything*," I said. "What is it Bob Villa's always saying about clutter? The best cure for clutter is to go *up* instead of *out*. Why don't you build some shelves?"

"Hey, Mom," nine-year-old Zachary said, as he raced to the top of the stairs to meet me. "Come on down. I've built a maze, and you'll *never* get through it." Then he disappeared down the stairs.

"Zach," I called after him, "I don't want to play in a maze right now. I just want to get to the kitchen for a relaxing cup of coffee." I followed after him, but he was already long gone.

The maze was there, though, just as he had said. It didn't look too complicated to me, so I began. First, I went through an opening made from stacks of old magazines, most of which I had ordered through the children's fund-raisers from school. Then I turned the corner and went past an ottoman stacked high with shoe boxes. "Zachary, these shoe boxes are supposed to be in the garage," I called out, hoping he could hear me— wherever he was. I moved on down the little shoe-box corridor until I came to a *T* and had to choose to go past either the last four issues of the Sunday paper or a basketful of socks that needed to be matched up and folded. "Zachary, I'm not kidding," I tried to sound more threatening. "I just want to get to the kitchen. You have some real cleaning up to do now!"

Zachary remained silent. So I chose the lane past the newspapers and traveled to a dead end at one of those pot carousels David hadn't hung from the ceiling yet. (I got a great deal on it at a flea market.) So I had to double back to the basket of unfolded socks, where I turned through a zigzag pattern of potted plants. (For a while there, if you bought $25 worth of groceries at Food Lion, you could have your pick of either a rhododendron or an African violet for only $6. Every house needs a little greenery.)

"Zachary, if you're looking to make some extra money," I said, "you can water these plants. Some are looking quite sickly." The maze led me through the dining room (where I hadn't intended to go), where I was forced to circle the dining room table because of the boxes of jigsaw puzzles (a very nice, therapeutic wintertime activity—we worked eight of them this winter alone). In the dining room I caught just a glimpse of Zachary peeping over a pile of old junk mail. (I hadn't had a chance to go through it and clip all the coupons yet.)

When I finally reached the kitchen, I pushed around some stuff on the counter: a can opener, a bread machine, a deep fryer, a salt and pepper shaker that looked like a butler and a maid (the butler—pepper—sneezes each time he's shaken, and the maid—salt—says, "Bless you!" Now, how could you throw something like that out?), some candleholders, a potpourri cooker, and a cutting board in the shape of Niagara Falls (it was a gift). I heated up the coffee, poured some in a cup that came from Mapco, and sat down on a stack of folded T-shirts I had collected from various special events (Mule Day in Columbia, Tennessee; Mark Lowry for President; National Spay and Neuter Awareness Week, etc.).

"Hey, darling," came a familiar voice.

I looked up to see Mom sipping a cup of coffee as well. "How long have you been here?" I asked.

"Oh, quite a while," she said. "Long enough to make about three trips through that maze. Zach may be a famous architect one day. He seems to have a real eye for getting the most out of a small space."

I took a sip of coffee and asked, "What's that thing you always used to say, Mom?"

"You mean about eating enough roughage so that—"

"No, no. That *other* thing you always used to say, you know, about clutter."

"Oh, yeah. I used to say, 'If you have a lot of clutter in your life, then you'll never be able to see all the important things ... because the clutter will sort of clutter things up so that everything looks ... cluttered.'"

"That's close enough."

"I used to be able to make that rhyme." She seemed a bit disappointed. Mom sort of drifted off in her thoughts (trying to recapture those rhymes, I imagined) while I thought about what she had said. Clutter can hurt (like my toe); it can strain a relationship (like Chera over her guitar); and it can block the most important things from our view (like Zach peeping over the junk mail).

"Do you know what I'd like to get?" I said to Mom.

"What?"

"A de-clutterer."

"Is there such a thing?"

"Got to be," I said, determined. "And when I buy one, I'm going to run it all through this house and get rid of every last bit of clutter."

"Think there might be one at the flea market?" Mom asked.

"Probably." I grinned.

"What do you think David will say?"

"The same thing he always says, 'Toss it out!'"

We just laughed and sipped more coffee. Mom went on to the flea market, but I went upstairs (back through the maze) and told my de-clutterer it was time to go to work. He rolled up his sleeves, and together, for the rest of the day, we simplified (tossed it out).

Anyway, that's how things look from up here.

DO WE REALLY HAVE TIME FOR A MILLION TV CHANNELS?

One day, when I was channel surfing and came across the Soddy Daisy vs. Hohenwald Checker Championship Game, I knew too many television channels were out there for too many people with too much time on their hands. So I started to think: Maybe these people don't realize how much time they spend watching television. That's when I came up with this idea for just one more channel—not a silly channel, either, but one that's definitely needed: the Time Channel. I even have a slogan for it already, "All Time, All the Time." Catchy, isn't it?

From anywhere in the world you could find out what time it is at home and what time it is where you're going tomorrow. In my mind I can see a small man, no bigger than a minute, with thinning hair, standing before a giant map of the United States. He waves an arm out over the West coast and says, "Right now this part of the country is experiencing the Pacific time zone, while our viewers in the East," as he pivots and switches arms so he can waft in that direction, "are steeped deep in the Eastern time zone."

He smiles a tiny smile as he continues, "Now let's take a look at the international time zone map." In the blink of an eye, the United States map is replaced with one of Europe. "As you can see, the present times range anywhere from 9 A.M. in Dublin, Ireland, to 5 A.M. in Ankara, Turkey. So if you're planning a trip anytime soon to Ankara, Turkey, please note that big difference in time zones." He isn't laughing, either. He doesn't seem the kind to make jokes about the time.

Then the little man stands at ease in front of Europe. "That's the international time report at this hour. Now let's take a look at the time in *your* local area."

The scene switches to a cheesy cardboard set where a man stands before a big digital clock, holding a long, wooden pointer. "Good evening, everyone," says the large, jolly man. "Boy, does time fly. It seems like only an hour ago I was standing here and telling you it was 8 P.M. Well, actually that *was* an hour ago, because now," and he raises the pointer up to the first digit of the digital clock, "it is exactly 9—*oops*, would you look at that—9:01 P.M. So if you're supposed to be in bed at nine, you're already late. That's a look at your local time. See you again in 59 minutes."

Yes, I'd be hooked on the Time Channel, all right. Someone would have to tear me away, mainly because time is always changing—and I would hardly be able to wait to see what would happen next.

In my mind I see the scene shift to a thin, mousy lady in a red suit sitting behind a walnut desk that's almost covered with the Time Channel logo (a big clock face whose hands are making swish marks because they are moving so fast). "Hello, I'm Patricia with your Time Channel News, and welcome to another segment of 'It's About Time.' The murder trial of a wealthy West Coast businessman tops our news tonight. This week the trial took an unexpected turn when a surprise witness brought new testimony to the courtroom."

The image of the anchorwoman dissolves slowly and is replaced by a gruff-looking man with a mustache. The graphic at the bottom of the screen identifies him as a juror.

"The case was pretty much open-and-shut," offers the juror. "Then a neighbor testified that she had been watching the Time Channel when she heard the gunshots and remembers that it was exactly 11:41 P.M." He shakes his head. "Time is time. You can't argue against *that* kind of evidence."

Patricia returns, looking stern and professional. "In other news," she continues, "a senior citizen woman credits the Time Channel with saving her life."

Instantly, a sweet woman with silver hair waves at the camera and says, "I'm on medication, so time is important to me. I watch the Time Channel all the time. I remember taking some medicine at 8:23 A.M. and then—I'm not sure how it happened, maybe it's the medication—I lost track of time." She shakes her head and bites her lip. "But the Time Channel was there for me. I just turned on the set, and it was exactly 11:32." Now she's weeping. "Two more minutes and it may have been too late. Thank you, Time Channel."

Patricia nods at the monitor in approval and then speaks right into the camera. "That's all the time I have for news about the time. Please join us next hour for 'It's About Time.'"

I'm weeping now. This is really good stuff.

The little man has changed to a light tan suit and is standing before a giant sundial. "Thanks for being with us tonight, folks. Now it's time that we take a look at the Big Clock." And there it is—a giant, simple clock with a big hand and a little hand. The little man continues to talk. "Let me remind you that what we're looking at here is the current Greenwich Mean Time. As you can see, the big hand is on the one, and the little hand is just a shade past the five. If you watch real close, you can actually see that big hand move. Zoom in, Jim, if you would—on the big hand—and give our audience a chance to see that hand better." Now the screen is filled with just the point of the big hand. And the announcer is right, you can actually *see* it creep by. I can actually watch time fly right past on the big, bright screen.

After a few minutes of this, the little man interjects, "All right. Thank you, Jim."

The camera shot pulls back, and once again you see the whole clock face. "As you can see," the voice-over continues, "it is now ten past the hour and won't be a quarter past for another ... oh, four-and-a-half minutes maybe. But don't worry, we'll keep you updated on the progression of this big hand throughout the night and into tomorrow."

I'm sort of sad, but I don't know exactly why. The clock disappears, and the little man is back, now standing before a small table covered with all sorts of clocks: digital, analog, wind-up, electronic, cuckoo. His smile quickly fades away as he announces, "Ladies and gentlemen, let's get serious for a moment. Tonight, as many of you are aware, daylight savings time will end at 2 A.M. Perhaps you are familiar with the cutesy little phrase, 'Spring ahead, fall back,' but tonight we're going to get beyond the veneer—the trivial—and discuss, with our Nobel Prize-winning expert, how this abrupt time change will affect each and every one of us and our families. Here before me," and he waves an arm over the collection of clocks, "are examples of many of the clocks you have in your own homes. Later we will work with each one, step-by-step, to demonstrate the proper way to set your clocks. Remember, folks, the Time Channel family is here for you. It's *time* you counted on us."

Time is so important, yet we take it for granted. Either that big hand moves fast or drags by slowly. Oftentimes I need something to remind me of time's passage—and this channel would help me. It would also help me to be aware of all the time I'm wasting (and the time it took to read this doesn't count!), all the times I have thought to myself, *I'll just do it later.*

Most of the time I waste is the time I spend worrying about time. I worry, for instance, about calling home when I'm traveling for my job, and waking everyone up when the time zones are not in our favor. But we have determined that talking to one another is one thing we never wait to do. Time won't stop so you can find a more convenient time to talk to your kids or hear your husband's voice. "I'll just do it later" seldom enters the conversation when we get an idea for a picnic (even if it's on the living room floor) or a walk around the block (even if we have to settle for a walk around the backyard).

Matthew 6:27 says it best: "Who of you by worrying can add a single hour to his life?" So stop worrying about time. Just be aware of it, appreciate it, make the most of it. Because if you forget, I'm going to send in my idea to the people who make up the cable TV stations. They'll think I'm a genius, and then you'll be stuck with something as stupid as the Time Channel.

Anyway, that's how things look from up here.

KIDS: THE ORIGINAL WORKOUT

People go to a lot of trouble to work out. Some will ride a bike for thirty minutes, climb steps for fifteen minutes, and run for another twenty. These are the people who can burn off enough calories to offset a dozen donuts, a lemon-filled eclair, and *three* bites of Death by Chocolate (using a tablespoon). These are people with no life.

And it doesn't matter how terrible they look, either. When they walk out of the gym all sweaty, sticky, messy, and often-times smelly, people will actually stop them to say, "Oh, you look wonderful!"—just because they know they've been working out. But if you happen to be sweaty, sticky, and wearing an Ann Taylor designer pantsuit, "wonderful" is not the word that would ever come to mind.

I'm talking about the truly obsessed people here—the ones who sleep with dumbbells. For a while there, I believed my sister-in-law Doris was one of those people. (Not because she sleeps with a dumbbell; I'm not trying to take a cheap shot at my brother, Mike!) No, I was suspicious because the other day, when she and I went to the YMCA to try out all the machinery, I finished up real quick, but Doris just kept going . . . and going . . . and going. (Like that little pink bunny.) I prayed for her for a couple of days before she confessed to me that she hadn't known how to turn off the Super-Duper Stair Hopper. What a relief—she wasn't one of those dumbbell people.

I saw something on TV the other day called the Body Sculptor. It looked more like a rose trellis, except the top parts curled over and dangled down, all fastened to a vinyl bench. The idea is that you sit down with your back to the trellis part, reach up and grab one of the half dozen arms hanging down in front of you, and either push or pull it while you watch TV or talk on the telephone. Almost immediately, a part of your body (depending on which arm of the trellis you grabbed) turns to steel. "But you want to pace yourself," the young man demonstrating warned. "Fine sculpting cannot be hurried."

The Body Toner 200 looked even better. The whole contraption is no bigger than a lunch box. The woman demonstrating hooked up to her legs six different cords held in place with patches that looked like those big, round Band-Aids for major wounds. When she threw the switch, each patch took turns sending a tiny (?) electrical current that made her legs twitch. (Sort of like I've seen frog legs do when they're fried up in a skillet.) Again, the beauty of this machine was that your body turned to steel while you watched TV or ate donuts.

Neither the Body Sculptor nor the Body Toner 200 is cheap. (Although they do offer their own financing—and a gift certificate for a dozen donuts.) But I have discovered another way to whip oneself into shape. It's not as easy as sitting in a chair and eating a donut, or flipping a switch and running up your electric bill, but it's cheap. As a matter of fact, it's free!

My girlfriend Angela and I got a good workout just the other day. She called me at seven in the morning and asked, "Are you dressed?"

"Blue spandex with a fuchsia, oversized sweatshirt," I answered.

"Oh, that color has always looked so good on you," she said.

"Thanks. How about you?"

"Well, I just bought one of those jogging outfits, the kind made from that slick parachute material."

"What color? Purple, I hope."

"Purple."

I squealed. "I bet you look *sooo* cute."

"Wait until you see me sweat."

"So, you're ready?" I asked.

"Yeah, come on over."

My kids were already in school, so I hopped in my van and headed over to Angela's.

When I arrived, I found she had started without me. She was lugging a car seat about the size of a small recliner out the front door. "I've got this, if you want to help Brittany," she called with a grunt. Brittany is her six-year-old daughter. (Angela's purple outfit did look great, and I told her so.)

Brittany still had her "sleepy" hair, so I grabbed a brush and pushed and pulled the bristles through the tangles. Then I twisted a rubber band around bunches of hair to make pigtails. "Looks good," I announced. "Now, go brush your teeth."

Just then her three-year-old brother, Austin, dashed past me in his stocking feet. Angela was close behind, wagging one shoe at him as she ran. I found the other shoe in the living room, picked it up, and fell in behind Angela, who was behind Austin, who was heading up the stairs. Angela took two steps at a time until she reached the very top, where she crawled the last few. I paced myself, feeling the stretch and strain of each hamstring. I caught up with her at the top, where we both collapsed to catch our breath.

"Did you see which way he went?" she asked.

I looked down the hall in both directions and shook my head. "You go that way, I'll go this way. If he makes a move for the steps, yell, and I'll head him off."

"Good plan."

We headed off in separate directions, both crawling for stealth—and because neither of us was ready to stand up just yet. I felt my lower abdominal muscles tighten with every baby crawl I took. Angela caught up with Austin at the foot of his Winnie the Pooh bed. Together we wrestled his shoes on him. Once we tied the laces, I stood and massaged my upper arms. That was tough.

"Okay," Angela announced, brushing her hair out of her face and fixing it back into the purple tie that matched her warm-up suit. "Is everyone ready to get in the van?" Austin took off like a shot, and we gave chase again. Down the stairs we went, my calves screaming out with every step.

Angela did five laps around the kitchen island before I took the baton and did four more. Then Austin swerved into the living room, and Angela swooped him up—just like we had planned. "Gotcha!" she said.

"I'll get the door," I panted.

"Meet you at the van," she said to me, holding Austin about the chest, his two feet squirming in all directions. Angela was holding on tight, biting her lip, reaching back for a little extra something that I'm sure she never knew she even possessed, her face turning a shade that came close to matching that of her suit.

She plopped Austin into his car seat, and together we tugged and pulled and cinched harnesses, braces, and straps. Brittany was so much easier, just pull and click the grownup seat belt. But her backpack weighed almost as much as Austin. I carried it from her upstairs bedroom and passed it off to

Angela, who lugged it down the back steps and rolled it into the van with a giant "Umph!"

We both stood there for a few moments, catching our breath and studying our handiwork. With the sleeve of my new shirt, I dabbed at the bead of perspiration on my forehead while Angela adjusted her hair. "Ready to roll?" she asked me.

"Ready," I said. "You drive."

The drive through the neighborhood wasn't too bad, a few turns here and there, a few stop signs. But once we entered the main highway, the story was different. Still, Angela handled the traffic like the seasoned mom she is. She worked the turn signal, pumped the brakes, and mashed the gas pedal. I noticed that whenever she gripped the wheel, like during a lane change, her knuckles would turn white. Then, at a stop sign or traffic light, they would flush back red as she loosened her grip.

We went to Brittany's school first. I hopped out, yanked open the van's side door, and unfastened Brittany, who skipped along the sidewalk and into the building. I squat-lifted her backpack and waddled in behind her.

When I got back to the van, Angela already had swapped seats with me. She was flexing both hands, rubbing away the tingles, and bringing back the circulation. "Your turn," she said to me with a smile.

I started out slow and easy, but then the right turn signal went out. "Got a burnout on the right!" I called over to Angela. She nodded and rolled down her window. I did the same. When we reached Austin's day care, which happened to be on the right, I stuck out my left arm and pointed back over the van. And, just in case whoever was behind me didn't understand what I was doing, I began to pump my arm up and down, like one of those lighted signs where the arrow seems to be moving across the side of a building. I looked over and saw Angela hanging out the passenger window, stabbing a finger into the air in the direction of Austin's school. I'm sure from behind we appeared very effective—fuchsia and purple arms flashing out from each side.

We made the turn safely and unbound Austin, taking turns carrying him to his classroom because he didn't want to walk. When we left the day care, Angela drove us to the mall. We walked past the fitness center, where a lot of people were dressed just like us. We found a place in the food court that sold chocolate donuts and coffee and snacked until the stores opened up.

Later we went shopping for some more workout clothes. I bought a chartreuse top with black piping and some spandex pants to match. (Angela said I looked like a frog, but I was also thinking about the burned-out turn signal in her van and how important it can be to be visible.) Angela bought this adorable, bright yellow fleece sweatshirt for 60 percent off. She looked like a canary, but it would help with the turning also. On our way out, we passed someone we recognized from church.

"Hello," our friend said. She was dressed in an Ann Taylor business suit and really could have tucked her shirttail in. (She looked a bit slouchy.)

"Hi," we both said, clutching our new purchases. My collar was still damp with sweat, and my muscles still ached from Brittany's backpack, so I walked with a slight hitch. Angela's hair had come out of the purple tie, and she was trying to push it out of her face.

Our friend looked at us, then glanced up at the fitness center sign behind us. As if she had it all figured out, she smiled and said, "You girls are looking just *wonderful!*" I wished we could have said the same about her. But it goes to show, you can get away with a lot of disasters if you wear a sweat suit.

We just giggled, thanked her, and told her she was crazy or blind or both. Then we headed back to the van, walking slowly, because school would be out pretty soon, and it seemed like a good idea to pace ourselves. After all, fine sculpting cannot be hurried.

Anyway, that's how things look from up here.

If I Were in Charge of Voice Menus

I had a great idea the other day. It came to me about ten minutes into a fifteen-minute wait on the telephone. I had just called the telephone company to add the call-waiting feature to my service. But when my ear began to ache (*and* my finger, too, from pushing all those buttons), I believed I had had enough call-waiting to last me for a long time and hung up.

That's when it hit me: Just think how much time I could save if I had some sort of calling menu on *my* phone. Why, I'd have time to do great things, like sleep. Or I could take up fun and creative hobbies, like sleeping. (It's not that I'm lazy, but if I had enough sleep, then I could do really, really great things, like clean my house.)

It took a long time to set up my menu selections since I had a lot of prerecorded messages to record. (Of course, they weren't prerecorded until *after* I had recorded them. But wouldn't that make them *post*recorded?) Anyway, once I had the system set up, I was so excited to see how it would work that the first day I just sat and listened to the calls come in.

Ring-Ring-Ring!

"Hello. This is Chonda. Welcome to my new voice menu system. I'm soooo excited about this and about the new freedoms and possibilities this brings to me as a working mother and wife and to you as someone who has lots of busy things to take care of and a desire to get on and off the phone as quickly as possible. To facilitate both our goals, please listen carefully to the following menu options and press firmly the button that most applies to the purpose of your call. I thank you from the bottom of my heart for being a big part of this new direction as I move into the new millennium. Just follow my directions. This will be easy, painless, and much faster than trying to call the water company just to ask how many days are in the current billing period."

I was trying to be light and humorous while at the same time taking a jab at what really gets my goat.

"If you would like to leave a simple message of twenty-five words or less for me, press one, now. If you have an even shorter message for David or the children, press two, now.

"If you are calling to make a delivery, press three, now. If you are calling to make a delivery but you are lost, press four, now.

"If you are my dentist calling to remind me of a cleaning I scheduled months ago and have simply forgotten all about, press 21, now, or if you've determined that a root canal is our only option, press 22, now.

"If you are calling to discuss the general happiness of my children, about their day in school, whether they've received all their shots and vaccinations, or about Zach's last report card, press 34, now.

"If you're calling because you don't think I'm raising my children correctly, you can hang up now.

"If you're calling because you'd like to go shopping, press 45, now.

"If you're calling because we went to high school together, and you haven't seen me in years, but you happened to see me on TV this week and thought I could get you free tickets to The Grand Ole Opry this Saturday night, press 59, now.

"If you've dialed the wrong number, press 16, now.

"If you're calling to see if I'd be interested in buying either bottled water or a security system for my home, press 44 and then quickly step away from your telephone.

"If this is someone from my small group at church reminding me of our next meeting, press 38, now. Or press 39 if you know for sure we are having snacks.

"If this is Zachary's principal, sorry about that overhead projector. Press 84 now to listen to a more formal apology.

"If this is someone from the Gallup Poll, press 53 if you favor a voice menu like this, 54 if you disapprove, 55 if you strongly disapprove, and 56 if you did not get this far into the message.

"If you've never liked the Beatles, press 41.

"If you'd like to start a recycling program in your neighborhood, press 81.

"If you are currently involved in, or have a desire to learn more about, a car pooling program for any grade-school children in the Barfield area, press 62.

"If we have ever been involved in the same car pooling program before, press 84 now to listen to a more formal apology.

"If you know of a good, quality facial soap that you would be willing to recommend, press 27.

"If you owe me any money at all, press 77, and I'll get right back with you.

"If you love chain letters, press 51, then press any three numbers at random and within a week you should receive at least a million phone calls from complete strangers.

"If you have any hot tips for *America's Most Wanted*, you'll have to press *66 and take an oath before continuing this call.

"If you have a hangnail that's been bugging you for some time, press 47. If it's a brand new hangnail, press 46.

"If you have a family member who has a problem with rhinoteleksemania, press 12. For a definition of rhinotelekse-mania, press 92. If you laugh, press 93.

"Mom, if that's you, press 67, then enter the number of times you have already called me this week and the percentage of those calls that have occurred before 7 A.M.

"If this is an emergency, press 69 and please hold for further instructions.

"If this message has made you late for any sort of meeting, press 84 to listen to a more formal apology.

"Thank you for your time and attention to these options. I wish only to make things convenient for you and myself—especially myself. As we continue to grow here, we will continue to update this menu, bringing you more and more options so that every need is met. If you would like to add other options, press 89 and leave some of your favorite numbers. If you'd like to talk with someone in person, that just won't be possible, so you'd better find a button to push. If you'd like to repeat this menu, press 99, now."

BEEP! Someone chose a button.

"Hello. This is Chonda. Welcome to my new voice menu system. I'm sooo—"

I snatched up the telephone, "Mom, is that you?"

"Hi, honey," Mom answered.

"Why are you listening to this again?"

"I didn't catch it all the first time," she said. "What was that you said about Zachary's principal?"

After a little bit, I found out that my mother had a doctor's appointment scheduled for the next day (I made a note to enter that as button 33 later), and she was a bit worried about going by herself and talking with the doctors who looked more at her chart, which was as fat as a phone book, than at her.

"I just like hearing your voice," she said. Taped or not, it didn't seem to matter to Mom. So I turned off the machine, and we talked for another hour. I guess I can put my house-cleaning on hold.

Anyway, that's how things look from up here.

IS THIS A
ROAD TEST?

The only way to explain the boxes of old baby clothes in my attic is to say that the day after Chera came home from the hospital, she grew up. Just like that. How could fifteen years have gone by so quickly? Yesterday I was rocking her to sleep—and today? Today I'm biting every fingernail on my right hand. (The left hand went during labor.) Because, at fifteen years of age, as every mother of teenagers or preteens knows, your baby obtains a driver's permit. (My prayer request should be obvious by now.)

Chera was only a few days past fifteen when we drove to the exam station. The room was full of parents (who looked older than I) and little children. But, as we waited our turn (for almost an hour!), I realized these little children, who were fifteen- and sixteen-year-olds, were coming together for one purpose and one purpose only: to make it legal for them to slip behind the wheel of their parents' car. (Whatever happened to the legislation that would move the driving age to, say, thirty-five—but only after the child had purchased said vehicle herself?)

Chera filled out the application and held it in one hand. In the other, she held a battered, rolled-up copy of the driver's manual she had been studying for the last several months. She was taking these last few minutes to study the shapes of signs and the various distances any driver is supposed to maintain when he or she is following someone, or there's a train crossing the street, or if it's wet or dry. As we waited, she was proud to rattle off all these numbers, measurements, colors, and shapes. For just a moment there, I was reminded of her earlier years, watching *Sesame Street* and getting so excited when she learned to tell a square from a triangle or the color blue from yellow.

The routine in this busy place quickly became apparent. First, we waited until our number was called. When it was our turn, we handed in the application. While Chera took a quick eye exam, I signed a piece of paper that stated I would be financially responsible for any damage Chera might do out on our public highways, at least until she was eighteen. Chera passed her vision test, and I added a little note to my sheet that this financial obligation would probably go on a lot longer than that.

I soon noticed that the other parents were experiencing varying degrees of uneasiness. Chera was there only to get a permit—just to take a test and that's it. But other kids were there for the real thing: a license. Their training was over. The parents of these kids seemed more anxious, more frightened, more sickly (you get the picture).

All the chairs were taken, so most of us stood in little clusters until every so often someone from the other side of the counter would call out a name. "Redmond! Testing station #4 is open." And a kid (I'm guessing a kid with the last name of Redmond) stepped out from the crowd and into an adjoining room where one long wall was lined with computer terminals.

The Redmond kid turned and gave a thumbs-up. Someone who looked just like him (only older) returned the thumbs-up.

"Johnson! Testing station #7 is open." Off went another future driver. She stopped long enough to smile and wave back at her mother. Her mother sort of giggled.

"Wilson!" came the voice from the other side of the counter again. "ROAD TEST!" This is when things changed. I saw Wilson step out from the crowd, and the parent of that child put a hand up to her mouth and gasp, as if she had just leaped into a pool of ice water. I could only watch, feeling a small portion of her pain, her anguish, her financial obligation, as she was put to the test. Her child, a young man with a fuzzy mustache (I *think* it was a mustache) sort of loped away the way only gangly teenagers can do, thumbs in his belt loops, shoulders bent over. He glanced back over his shoulder and forced a grin at his mom, as if to say, "Gee, Mom, cool it. Everything's rad, so take a chill pill. It's just a road test." But I could tell, as a parent, that would be a hard pill to take. I looked at Chera, but she hadn't noticed anything; she was trying to recall the maximum jail time for first- and second-time DUI convictions.

Chera was sent to testing station #2. I stood in the corral with the rest of the parents and watched her push different spots on the computer screen as she answered the questions, trying to imagine her behind the wheel of the family van. She was supposed to answer thirty questions, missing no more than six—but after twenty-four, the machine stopped and dismissed her. She stood up and walked out to me, a bit stiff from nerves, and said, "I think I got them *all* right."

"All of them?" I said (but I shouldn't have been surprised). "You mean, it didn't beep or buzz or anything like that?"

She shook her head. "No. Actually, it was quite easy. And most of them were common sense, like, if you cross the street at night you should (a) wear light-colored clothes; (b) wait until the sun comes up; or (c) cross in front of big trucks."

I wondered if people who missed this question ever drove through my neighborhood.

As Chera realized that one tough part was over and she wouldn't have to carry that old, battered driving manual around anymore, she also figured out that the toughest part was yet to come: the picture. She combed her hair and practiced smiling. "How does this look?" she asked, flashing a perfect smile.

"Tilt your head a bit this way," I said, feeling I had to give her *some* instruction or she wouldn't believe me.

Even though she looked beautiful, and even though the testing instructor had to show her perfect score off to everyone there at the counter, Chera took one look at her driver's permit photo and said, "It's makes my head look squished."

I just smiled and said, "They only get worse."

I let her drive on the straight road home. We hadn't gone very far when we approached a van going in the other direction with its turn signal on. Chera came to a quick and complete stop, almost standing on the brakes.

"What are you doing?" I asked. The thought of that form I'd signed earlier flashed through my mind.

Just then another car pulled up from a side street. Chera rose from her seat a little so she could mash the brakes down even farther. Both the people in the van and the car stared at us. I stared at Chera. "I'm yielding! I'm yielding!" she shouted, her knuckles white around the steering wheel.

"But, Chera, you have the right of way," I said, trying not to get too excited so she wouldn't get too excited. After a few moments of this, the guy in the van threw his hands up in frustration, not sure what to do.

"The book says never assume you have the right of way!" Chera said.

The guy in the car waved a thank-you—as if we were being polite—and shot out in front of us. Finally the guy in the van got tired of Chera's "yield" and turned in front of us.

"But you can't yield when everyone else is yielding to you," I explained.

Chera looked at me with a determined expression. "I can out-yield anyone!" And then she added, "As long as I'm *two* car lengths away. Now, do I turn here or go straight?"

I imagined my expression must have been the same as the woman's back at the testing station whose son loped off to take a road test. Here was my baby girl, the one who had gotten car sick and thrown up as little child on the backseat of this very van, the one who had left crayons to melt in the sun on the backseat of this very van, the same one who had eaten dozens of Happy Meals on the backseat of this very van. And now she was behind the wheel, mashing the gas, standing on the brake, and yielding on busy highways.

A year from now, I thought, *we'll probably be back in that same testing station, and someone from the other side of the counter will call "Pierce, ROAD TEST!" and Chera will lope off to show what she can do on the highway (maybe even parallel park) while I twist my face into expressions that will alarm other parents watching me.*

So I am determined that we will practice every day. She will become comfortable with the gas, the brakes, the turn signals, the seat belts, the wipers. She will know when to slow down and when to accelerate, how to merge and how *not* to merge. And most important, I will teach her when to yield and when *not* to yield. She will be able, when the day of the road test comes, to pass the test.

But then again, since the day she was born, we've been preparing her for her real ROAD TEST. And that test, one long and seemingly endless test, has nothing to do with cars.

Anyway, that's how things look from up here.

My All-Time Favorite Wedding— Most Definitely

I love to go to weddings. I love the lace, the chiffon, the satin, the wire ties that keep flowers from flopping over, the cuff links, the organ music, watching the back of the bride's and groom's heads for a half-hour, the rice (or confetti or birdseed), the shoe polish, the candelabras, the ribbons (lots of ribbons), and the patent leather shoes. I love all this, especially when I know the family.

But once I went to the wedding of a fourth cousin (twice removed) that was a celebration of a different kind. Everything started off pretty normal. The church was decorated with long, skinny candles that dripped wax all over the carpet, and the organ player banged out some old Martin Luther hits.

Then, at the end of "A Mighty Fortress," the lights went out. I heard a few people gasp with surprise. Almost instantly, a spotlight beamed down on center stage, and there stood a man in a tuxedo with a ruffled shirt. In a shaky voice, he started to sing the theme from the *Titanic*. (I know it's pretty music, but I wondered if my fourth cousin—twice removed—ever thought about the context of that song and whether it would be appropriate for a wedding.) Despite the singer's chronic vibrato, his presentation was nice, moving from one side of the platform to the other, the spotlight following right along with him. At the conclusion of his song, we all clapped. It seemed like the appropriate thing to do.

After that, the house lights came back up, and three young ladies (had to be sisters) stepped up on the stage. One of them had strapped a guitar across her shoulder. They surrounded a single microphone, and the one with the guitar began to strum a toe-tapping little folk tune. I'd never heard the song before, but it was about a man who loved a woman so much that he sold his horse and worked on the railroad for twenty years and saved his money. Then he joined the Foreign Legion for a season, and when he returned to this country, he finally found his true love. But as he was walking across this hot, burning plain (without his boots because he had given them to someone less fortunate), he was killed by a buffalo stampede right in front of his true love, who hadn't seen him in thirty years but still recognized him as her true love because he had lost one of his little toes as a kid when he had saved her life by fighting off a pack of wild wolves. At the end of the song, I noticed several people crying (those who weren't asleep).

The trio received a smattering of applause as well. Then the organist played something from *Dr. Zhivago*, or at least it sounded Russian, and the lights dimmed again. This time some dancers (Russian? Arabian? Pentecostal? It was hard to tell.) came onto the stage from both sides, swinging purple scarves and doing figure eights around the candelabras. The people who had fallen asleep during the folk song were wide awake now. (The flowing scarves were coming awfully close to the candles.) This went on for some time, and I was just beginning to make out a story, kind of like watching an Italian opera, when one of the dancers picked up another one, and they both fell over in a heap beneath a red spotlight. The power of love? Love conquers all? Don't pick up someone heavier than you are? I knew a message was in there somewhere, but I'm not real sharp about these kinds of things. Someone up front started to clap, and we took that to figure the dance was over, so the rest of us clapped, too.

Then a man stepped onto the platform, who I figured was the emcee. (Later I found out he was the pastor performing the ceremony of my fourth cousin—twice removed.) The spotlight was so bright the man had to squint.

"Ladies and gentlemen," he said, in a voice that sounded like Ed McMahon back when he was hosting *Star Search*. "We have one more performance for you tonight. Rodney's great-aunt Martha..." (Rodney? I thought his name was Randy!) "... will now conduct an interpretive reading of an original poem."

Then the emcee (pastor) bowed out of the spotlight, and a tiny woman with a plastic binder took his place. She laid her notebook on the podium, took a long, slow drink from the glass stationed there, cleared her throat, and began.

"Alone.
Lonely.
Aha. There you are.
Holding hands.
Buying pizza.
Got five dollars I can borrow?
Meet my family.
Tell some jokes.
Ha-ha-ha-ha!
I need to ask you something.
Yes.
The beginning."

With this last line delivered, Aunt Martha grabbed up her binder, stepped away from the podium, and gave a long, deliberate bow (as if she had some experience before a live audience). She received the greatest applause yet. (And lots of *ooohs* and *ahhhs* from the sentimentalists.)

The pastor took over the podium, and with a cueing wave of his hand, the organist pounded out the "Wedding March." My fourth cousin and his buddies entered from a side door, and his fiancée marched elegantly down the center aisle, arm-in-arm with the man who had sung the theme from *Titanic* earlier. The ceremony and the exchange of vows seemed like any other wedding I had been to. (Although it seemed that a lot of different people lit a lot of different candles so that the whole room glowed with evidence of the symbolism of each—whatever that symbolism might have been.)

And I have to admit, when Randy—I mean, Rodney—said, "I do," I cried like a baby. I probably would have cried a lot longer if the groomsmen hadn't followed after him on unicycles, throwing birdseed. (The bride threw her bouquet and caught one of the unicyclists in the side of the head and tipped him over, but he landed in the coatrack so he was okay.)

The light man turned on the mirror ball, and some people hung around to listen to the bride's dad sing "I Will Always Love You" (someone really should have talked to him about his song selections). But most of the audience hurried on over to the reception—at the laser tag place down the road. (Rodney's new wife is a great shot!)

I still love weddings. And I don't think any wedding would be complete without loads of chiffon. But every time I go to a wedding now (I have some third cousins on my mom's side who are getting to that age), I miss the lights, I miss the drama, I miss the unicycles.

Anyway, that's how things look from up here.

IF I CAN REMEMBER THE NAME OF THE DOCTOR OF MY SUNDAY SCHOOL TEACHER'S NEPHEW'S BEST FRIEND'S MOTHER, WHY CAN'T I REMEMBER WHAT DAY THIS IS?

Nothing beats having a good memory. I've always envied those people who do. Dates, people, places, names—first and last—are all at their disposal. Those are the kind of people who could live their entire lives without a Daytimer. My cousin, Thad Lee, can remember every person's birthday on our entire family tree.

My mom's like that. She can remember everything—as long as it didn't happen in the last couple of weeks. The farther back you go, the better she can remember. One of my favorite things to do is to have Mom over early in the morning (after 9:00 A.M., Mom, if you're reading this) to share a cup of coffee with me and just talk about what's going on in our lives—old things and new.

She only lives a couple of miles away, so we visit often. The other morning she came over and wanted to tell me about Rev. Carrol's wife, Myrtle. "You remember her, don't you?" she asked. "When we were living in Kentucky, she would come over just about every week and bring you girls cookies."

"I was five years old when we lived in Kentucky," I said.

"Yeah, anyway, I ran into Sue McMillian, who knows the Jarrells—you know, the ones with the pet pig—and they said they ran into the Boyds, who own the little junk store in Peagram—the one where the Millers bought the old chair that broke on Mrs. Miller, and she had to go to the hospital for stitches, remember that? Anyway, they read in *The Standard*, you know, the church magazine, that Myrtle got shingles and nearly died."

"You don't say?" I said, as I prepared our coffee.

"Oh, yes. You know, the same thing happened to Gretta Peach."

"Really?"

"Yes. Nearly killed her. You know, she used to ride a bike to work every day. Six miles one way. But she had to quit."

"Work?"

"No, the bike. Shingles nearly killed her. Honey, I didn't know you took cream in your coffee. Anyway, her son drove her to work when she got better. I wonder if he's married yet. I'll have to call Mae Philson to find out."

"Mae?"

"Yes, Gretta still sends Mae a Christmas card every year, and sometimes she'll drop in a little note to tell everyone how she's doing. That's how I knew Myrtle had shingles."

"I thought Sue McMillian read it in *The Standard*."

Mom shook her head. "Oh, no. Sue knows Betty Ralston, who knows Mae Philson, who gets one of these cards from Gretta. That's where I learned about Myrtle's shingles—long before it ever came out in *The Standard*. I just figured I'd break the news to you myself before you heard it from anywhere else—now that it's gone public." She took a sip of her coffee as she kicked around another thought. "Someone else had shingles," she said. "Got 'em young, too. But I can't think of her name now." Mom looked about the room. "Something's different here, isn't it?"

"Well . . ."

"Don't tell me. Let me guess." She looked about the living room, then the kitchen, until her eyes settled on me. "Hmmm," she mused.

"Maybe it's the new painting over the mantle," I offered. "I don't think you've seen it."

"You have a new painting?"

"Yeah. After David knocked a hole in the wall, it was easier to cover the hole with a painting than to try to patch it."

"Louise Mantooth."

"Louise who?"

"Mantooth. Louise Mantooth. That's the name of the girl who had shingles when she was only sixteen. I knew her well. Liked to scare me to death because I was sixteen, too. No, shingles is not just for old folks. Louise also had this big mole behind her ear that was horrible. I'd always tell her she should have that thing lopped off. No, the painting's not it. There's something else. You had a hole in the wall?"

"Yes. David was using a hammer to take up the old carpet when the hammer flew out of his hand and shot right through the sheet rock. I thought I'd die." I giggled. "Of course, looking back now, it was kind of funny."

Mom drank her coffee and said, "Oh, so you bought new carpet?"

"Yeah, we had to because we couldn't get that bloodstain out of the old one."

"Bloodstain?"

"Yes, David stepped on a nail when we were tearing down the wall in the living room to build the new archway to connect the living room with the dining room," I explained. "He hopped around all over the place and messed up the carpet. He's okay now."

Mom took a sip of coffee and studied the expansive archway for the first time. "You mean a wall used to be there?"

"Well, only up until recently. I wanted to recover the sofa, but when David and his buddies tried to carry it out, the sleeper unfolded and smashed into the doorframe. That took care of most of the demolition."

Mom looked at the sofa in the living room. "You just had that recovered?"

"Yes. It was kind of a project for the whole class."

"What class?"

"The upholstery class I took."

"When did you take an upholstery class?"

"A long time ago," I said. "I stepped down as president of the International Upholsterers Society just last week. I'm sorry I forgot to tell you. Just a figurehead position, really. Raised money, picketed sweatshops in Central America, lobbied Congress—things like that." (Central America didn't faze her!)

Mom studied the sofa. "No, that's not it, either."

"Of course, I wouldn't have had it recovered if the firemen had just listened to me when I told them that everything was under control," I said. "But nooo, they had to hose down the upstairs anyway."

"You had a fire?"

"Just a small one. I had it out by the time they arrived. Zach was doing some kind of science experiment."

"Zach?"

"Zachary, my son."

"Oh, Zachary, yes, of course." She held up her cup. "Can I bother you for some more coffee?"

I poured some for both of us and said, "Of course, you can't tell where Chera backed the car into the house from in here so it couldn't be that."

"So Chera's driving, huh?" she said.

"Only on the days when her father has to be in court."

"Court?"

"Yes, he's on jury duty this month."

She seemed somewhat relieved at that explanation, and I apologized for scaring her that way.

By now I was as curious as she was to discover what Mother believed was so different. "I know!" I said, as I pulled back my hair. "My new earrings. David bought them for me when he was being held hostage in Madagascar—well, not *while* he was a hostage. But shortly after the successful negotiations were conducted by the United Nations." I turned my head sideways so she could see them better. "They were sort of a coming home present for me."

Mother studied the earrings for a moment, and then her face lit up as bright as my newly painted kitchen (which I had forgotten to tell her about). She reached out and stroked my hair. "Why, you got your hair cut, didn't you?"

I nodded. "Yes, Mom. But that was more than six months ago."

"It looks so good, honey."

"Call Angela," I offered. "She'll tell you. Six months, really. I haven't even had it trimmed since."

Mom sipped her coffee and grinned, pleased with herself for figuring out the change. "I do believe it makes you look slimmer."

"But . . ." Instead of saying anything else, I pulled the hair back over my earrings and adjusted a curl or two. "Slimmer? You think so?"

Mom nodded. "Hey, you remember Bertha Hampton, don't you? She's the one who fell off the curb in front of Wal-Mart and that lawyer fellow, Stuart Wilson, who was in love with Amy Mae Rogers from Elizabethtown, said he would take the case on for free, but Bertha got food poisoning at the Sonic and . . ."

I love sharing a cup of coffee with Mother and talking about what's going on in our lives.

By the way, all the names in this chapter have been changed to protect my mother, as well as the nice UN negotiators, the citizens of Madagascar, and the lobbyists representing Central America. And, Myrtle, get well soon.

Anyway, that's how things look from up here.

CHATTING WITH MARTHA STEWART ABOUT MY TO-DO LIST

Last night I had another dream about Martha Stewart. She showed up at my house early in the morning, just after the kids had gone to school. We sat in my huge sunroom (which I don't have in real life—that's how I knew it was a dream) and talked like old girlfriends while a small jazz ensemble played in a far corner, by the fountain that had real koi fish swimming about and several thousand dollars in change underwater where people had stopped to make a wish. Martha and I were sipping our coffee. (Just some cheap, decaffeinated stuff I had bought at Kroger's.)

"So your kids are in school?" she asked.

"Oh, yes. Long ago," I answered.

"Children are so cute," she said, sipping her coffee. "I would love to have watched them make their own breakfasts and prepare their own lunches to take."

"Me, too."

"You mean, you didn't watch them?"

"I mean, they didn't make their own breakfasts, let alone their own lunches."

She set down her coffee cup slowly and said, "You mean, you prepared for both of them?"

"*And* myself *and* my husband."

"Oh, my." Her forehead wrinkled.

"Oh, Martha, enough about that. I've been dying to ask you something. On that show you did last Christmas, did you really make your own salt and pepper?"

Martha cut a glance about the room to make sure we were alone (with the exception of the jazz ensemble and the fish, of course). Then she confided, "I have to be honest."

I leaned in closer.

"Someone else quarried the salt."

"No!"

She nodded. "Of course, I grew and harvested the pepper and ground it myself. *And* I filled the shakers." She smiled and seemed pleased with herself. She nodded her approval to the jazz ensemble and then looked about the room. "This is such a lovely room. Did you make it?"

"Oh, heavens no. Are you kidding? I just dreamed this thing up. I have so much laundry to do, when would I find time to make glass and glue it together like you would?"

"Laundry? What do you mean by laundry?"

"You know, separating the darks from the whites, the towels from the delicates."

"Then what?"

"Then I put them in the washer, add soap—"

"I can make soap."

"—make sure all the socks are turned right-side-out—"

"All of them?"

I nodded. "And then dry."

"Dry?"

"And fold."

"Fold?"

"And put away."

"Where?"

"Why, into the proper chest of drawers or closet. Or at least neat little stacks in the corner of the room."

"I hadn't thought about that. So how long does a job like that last?" she wanted to know.

I paused for a long moment—for effect, I admit, and to give her an opportunity to swallow her last drink of coffee—before saying deliberately, "*Forever.*"

She put a hand to her mouth, and I feared maybe I hadn't paused long enough. "I hadn't thought about that," she said.

"Oh, please," I said, "enough about laundry. Do tell me about that crumpet party I saw on your show once."

"Crumpets are boring," she said.

"Then tell me about how you made your own paper for the invitations."

She dismissed this with a wave and said, "Just like any other paper—wood pulp, et cetera." Then, lowering her cup from a fresh swallow, she asked, "Have you ever vacuumed your carpet?"

I nodded.

"I mean, like a *whole* room?"

"Try a whole house," I said, trying not to sound as if I were bragging.

She gasped.

"And then I usually dust," I added.

"Dust what?"

"The furniture."

"I can build furniture," she said.

"I know, Martha, and you're quite good."

Just then the phone rang, and I answered, "Oh, yes, I'm expecting you. I'll be here with Martha Stewart. . . . Okay, I'll ask." I covered the phone and asked Martha, "The plumber wants to know why the hot water valve is always on the left and cold on the right."

"Tell him," Martha said, "to watch this Sunday's program."

"Watch her this Sunday," I said into the phone. "Besides, this is *my* dream, and I'm having my *own* chat." I hung up and said, "That was the plumber. He'll be here in a bit."

"Plumber? For what?"

"Toilet's stopped up."

She set down her coffee and pushed it away from her. "How do you do it?"

"Do what?"

"Take care of your children, husband, do the laundry, vacuum, dust the furniture, take out the trash—you do take out your own trash?"

"Only when it's full."

"And *then* cook?"

I nodded, but I had never thought of my day as quite so overwhelming, so daunting a task, until I heard Martha Stewart lay it out so plainly.

I shrugged and said, "Practice, I guess."

The plumber showed up, gave Martha a big hug, and told her how great her spinach quiche recipe was. He dragged out a big coiled cable with a giant electric motor that uncoiled the cable across the room and into my toilet. After a few moments, the plumber spun it backwards and pulled out Bongo, my son's favorite Beanie Baby.

"So *that's* where that went!" I said, spraying it down with some Shout and dropping it into the washer, which was set for the very next load. Zach would be so excited when he came in from school.

The plumber asked for Martha's autograph (on an old nasty plunger of all things), picked up his auger and left.

I retrieved a mop from the garage and wiped up some size thirteen prints from the vinyl floor.

"*Why* do you do this?" Martha asked, the exasperation evident in her voice.

"Do what?"

"All this," and she waved an arm about my big sunroom, but she meant my whole house. "The laundry, the dusting, the vacuuming, the mopping—"

"Don't forget the windows."

"You do windows? *Why?* Couldn't you just hire someone to take care of menial tasks like these so you would have more time for other things, like weaving napkins with an interlaced monogram, or crafting reproductions of Early American Shaker furniture?"

Now that the plumbing seemed to be taken care of, I filled Martha's cup with more coffee. The dark liquid warmed the cup; sunshine poured through the glass overhead and warmed everything else. I noticed the streaks and the dust, so I added "clean the sunroom" to my to-do list. I'd take care of it as soon as Martha left.

I carried the pot of coffee back to the kitchen and dragged the mop behind me, thinking about Martha's question. The jazz ensemble was playing something perky now as I answered her. "Perhaps in *your* dreams things like that can happen, Martha, but not in mine."

Glancing at my watch, my heart thumped. Any minute my kids would be barreling in the door looking for an after-school snack. I pulled a box of Little Debbie snack cakes out of the cupboard and laid them on a plastic plate. No, I didn't make them myself, but the kids wouldn't care. They would be too busy ripping open the wrappers, and I would be too busy hearing about their day. I'm pretty comfortable with that. Suddenly I felt a little sad for Martha.

On the way past the fountain, I flipped in a quarter and made a wish.

Anyway, that's how things look from up here.

THIS MEANS
W.W.H.A.R.

My washer and dryer have been broken for months. Actually, they have been partly broken for years; it was only a couple of months ago that they became fully broken—at least as I define *broken*.

David hasn't gone that far yet; he claims they're just a bit *moody*. "Look," he tells me, when the washer stops in midcycle, "if you just raise the lid—not all the way, mind you, three-quarters will do it—let it drop, and *voila!* She works." I hate it when he speaks French, especially when he's talking about the appliances.

"But what if I'm not here to raise and drop the lid so it can *voila*?" I shot back.

"Then we train the children," he said. "We'll teach them to run reconnaissance into the washroom every ten minutes during heavy wash periods—"

"Which is every day," I interjected.

"—lift the lid and drop. They're fast learners. They'll catch on. A few years ago, when this problem first started, I wouldn't have considered this tactic, but Zach's old enough now to reach the lid."

"And what about the dryer?"

"What about it?"

"After a couple of loads, it won't come on. It overheats, you say. Isn't that dangerous?"

"Well, if it didn't shut off, yes. That's why that safety valve is there—to shut it down. If you let it cool for a bit, then push the start button—"

"I know, I know, *voila!*"

"Exactly."

When I explained this scenario to a friend of mine, Sally, she invited me to a little support group she was involved in called W.W.H.A.R., or Women Whose Husbands Avoid Repairs.

"Thousands of us are out there, Chonda," she said. "Maybe even millions. Come see what we do."

I didn't have anything else to do. (The children had perfected their lift-drop method so well I was no longer needed in the laundry room.) So I went.

Four of us met at Betty's house, the host for the evening, in her living room. I found a seat on her sofa, and Betty brought out some coffee and cakes.

"Such a lovely home," I told Betty. "Thank you for inviting me."

She smiled warmly, offered me a cake, and said, "You might want to scoot to this edge of the sofa." She pointed to the opposite end from where I was seated. "The leg broke off that end a few years ago, and I have a couple of catalogs under it now. Sometimes it wobbles, and it's not very trustworthy."

I took the cake and slid over as she suggested.

Sally was there and was sitting in a big, wing-backed chair across from me. Another woman was named Rose. She was rather quiet and hadn't spoken yet. Sally took charge and brought the meeting to order. Then she introduced me. "She has a sad, sad story," Sally said, referring to me. "Chonda, why don't you tell them what you told me."

I couldn't hide my confusion. "Okay, well . . . when I was four, I had this cat—"

"No, no. Not *that* story. The one about the washer and dryer."

All the other women nodded, as if that explained a lot already. So I told them the whole story, all the seamy details about dropping the lid and waiting out the dryer and David's poor French. I'd never seen such a sympathetic group. Betty kept repeating little phrases like, "That's right," "I can't believe that," "Isn't that something?" Sally would keep me on track if I left out some details I had shared with her earlier but had forgotten for the group. The woman named Rose even shed a tear. I believed I was striking a chord with this group.

When I finished, they applauded me. (I believe they were applauding my courage.) With all the coffee and the cakes and the empathizing, the room started to heat up. Betty rose to flip on a switch for the ceiling fan. She looked up at the fan, but nothing happened. Then, with a balled-up fist, she rapped the switch twice—just like Fonzie used to do to that jukebox on *Happy Days*. She looked at us apologetically and said, "Phil says the switch has a loose connection. Twice is the most I ever have to whack it, though."

My friend Sally went next. In this small group setting, she opened up like I'd never heard her before. " . . . and I have to stick a butter knife in the garage door opener to make it work . . ."

"I can't believe that," said Betty.

" . . . and whenever we flush the toilet, we have to take that back lid off and jiggle something. I'm not sure what it is, but it's all wet and clammy in there. Tom just says to jiggle it. And because of that," now her voice cracked, "I can't display my little ballerina collection like I used to."

Rose began to bawl. I could see now why they invited her.

Betty went next. Most of her woes we had already lived through here in the living room, with the catalogs under her sofa and the whack-on, whack-off ceiling fan. But the most recent devastating development in her life had to do with the icemaker: "When it fills up with water, it makes the most embarrassing sound, and Phil and the boys will just laugh and laugh. I can live with the temperamental fan, but I *cannot* live with *that*."

I could have sworn I saw Rose grin, but she covered her mouth so quickly with her tissue that I couldn't be sure.

"Thank you all for sharing today," Sally spoke. "And how about you, Rose? How are things at your house?"

Rose only nodded, as if to say, everything's fine.

"Is Ed still lighting the gas grill with a paper torch he lights from the oven?" Betty asked.

Rose nodded.

"And instead of fixing the garbage disposal," Sally added, "does he drive five miles to the landfill to get rid of the table scraps?"

Rose nodded again.

"Well, I think we've had a good, productive meeting," Sally said, preparing to adjourn for the evening. Then Rose spoke up for the first time.

"I have a confession to make," she said, rather meekly.

Silence. What a good night to join the group, I thought, just as one of the members spills out a major confession. I leaned forward on the edge of the sofa, conscious of the catalogs holding up the other end.

"Do you remember how I told you my blender won't puree?" she asked. "That it'll only mince and grate if the vegetables aren't too fresh?"

Betty and Sally nodded, and Betty said, "That's right."

"Well, I came home yesterday, and Larry had bought me a new blender," she grinned, but it quickly turned into a happy sob.

"A new blender!" Sally, Betty, and even I said in unison. This was indeed unheard of in this group.

"What did you do, Rose? Nag him?" Betty asked.

She shook her head.

"Stay at your mother's for a few days?" Sally said.

Rose shook her head again.

"Ah," Betty said with a knowing grin, "you had your mother stay with *you* for a few days."

Again Rose shook her head.

"Well, what then?" Sally was becoming impatient. "Borrow his razor? Burn his food? Develop a headache?"

Rose just shook her head. Now she was grinning through her tears as she said, "I just *asked* him for a new blender."

More silence. I could tell the women of W.W.H.A.R. had never thought of this tactic. "So you expect us to believe," said Sally, "that you simply said, 'Hey, Larry, the old blender's broken. Can we get a new one?' And he did? Just like that?" She snapped her fingers.

Rose nodded. "Just like that," she said, and she snapped her fingers.

After a reflective pause, Sally finally said, "Well, I guess we'd better adjourn. We'll meet next week at my house. Remember, the doorbell is broken, so when you push the button, make sure you pull it back up. Last time, the cat was traumatized for a month."

"Ah, Sally," Rose said, "I don't think I'll be able to make it."

"Why not?"

"Larry and I are going shopping for a can opener—one with a magnet to catch the lids." She giggled.

So went my first meeting with W.W.H.A.R.

A few days later, as I wrestled a basket of dirty laundry from the upstairs bedrooms, I caught David lifting and dropping the lid on the washer. (That's his job when the kids are in school.) He gave a satisfactory nod as the agitator kicked in and soapy water began to churn. He then turned his attention to the dryer, turning and tweaking some knobs, but nothing happened. Finally, he gave it a sharp rap on the control panel, and the drum began to roll.

"So we have to hit the dryer now?" I said.

He turned to me with a satisfied grin. And that's when I understood. The male psyche feels a sense of victory at being able to set something in motion—no matter if he has to hit, whack, rap, or kick it. Every time Fonzie hit the jukebox, the lights would flash, some slow, romantic dance tune would start to blare, and girls would squeal with delight. Men think that women like to see them make things work that way.

Well, maybe that's okay for a jukebox, but it ain't the same with a washing machine. I wasn't ready for a full-blown war here, so I thought I'd try Rose's approach.

"Why don't we get a new washer and dryer?" I asked, dropping the heavy load of laundry at his feet.

His smile dissolved slowly, and I thought I could almost see his train of thought shift tracks to a track he had never even considered. Once the train was up and going again, he said, "Yeah, I guess we could do that. That might be a good idea. How about Monday night?"

That sounded great to me. That also happened to be the night Rose and Larry were going can opener shopping. I'd call Sally and tell her I wouldn't be able to make it to the next meeting, either.

It's a powerful weapon, communication. At least, it put an end to this W.W.H.A.R.

Anyway, that's how things look from up here.

Seriously, Sometimes We Take Life Way Too Seriously

I recently read somewhere (in a scholarly journal, I believe) that to be the most productive, the most creative we can be, some fun time must be included in our schedules. A big dose of play "doeth good like a medicine" it said. (Perhaps I was perusing a medical journal when I read this.)

WHOOPEEEEEEE!

I was so glad because *I'm* the one who, while speaking at a conference in which a woman was doing sign language for the deaf, slipped up behind her and said as fast as I could, "Supercalifragilisticespialidocious!" You should have seen the looks on the faces of those who heard me. Stunned. Shocked. Soured. However, all the deaf people cracked up.

Have you ever met people who just need to lighten up a little? I have; every crowd has at least one. (Why do they always have to sit in the front row?) They are the ones who need to laugh or they'll dry up and blow away. (That's not just me speaking, but also the scholarly, medical, scientific, Nobel Prize-winning article I read.)

One of those people was a waitress who waited on me not long ago.

"Are you ready to order?" she asked.

"Sure, I'll have the same thing I had last time," I said.

"I don't know what you had last time."

"Okay. Then I'll order something different." I waited but didn't see even a smile—not even a fake one. I know it wasn't the funniest thing anyone had ever said, but it should have made her smile. Instead, she just stood there with her pen hovering over her blank order book, looking over the top of it and waiting for me to continue.

So I tried again. I asked, "Do you have soup de jour?"

"Yes, we do. It's clam chowder."

"No, I mean just plain soup de jour."

Not even a twitch from the corner of her mouth. What was wrong with this woman?

"I'll have the clam chowder," I said. "But put it in a large milk glass and bring me some extra straws."

She nodded and wrote down the order. Before she could get away, I added, "And can you hold the clams, please?"

She scratched down the instructions and said, "Very well, ma'am. Thank you, and I'll be right back with your bread."

Like I said, some people just need to lighten up. Take the police officer who pulled me over not long ago. "Ma'am, do you know why I stopped you?"

"Because you're lost?" I asked, but as soon as that left my mouth, I wished I hadn't said it because he yanked his ticket book from his hip pocket as if to say, *"Wanna play tough, huh, lady?"*

"I clocked you doing 45 in a 40-mile-an-hour zone," he said. "That's a fifty-dollar ticket."

"How much is 35 in a 30-mile-an-hour zone?" I asked. "Because I was doing that earlier, and if it's cheaper . . ."

I kind of wished I'd kept that one to myself, too, because now he started to write. "Let me see your license," he said.

I dug it out of my purse and handed it to him. "This is a really bad likeness," I apologized for the picture on the license as I handed it to him. "I had sinus problems that day. That's why my face appears so swollen."

He kept writing, copying numbers from my license to his ticket book. So I asked him, "So what do you think about Ricky Shroeder taking over as captain on *NYPD Blue*?"

No answer.

"Do you know it's against the law to wear sunglasses after dark in Seymour, Oregon?" I informed him.

Still no response. Instead, he handed me the ticket book and asked me to sign—not an admission of guilt, he clarified, just that I received the ticket. "My real name? Or my alias?" I asked and right away wished I hadn't.

He frowned. What was wrong with him? So I signed my name and gave him his ticket book back; he gave me my fifty-dollar ticket. As he walked away, I called out, "Tell Andy I said, 'Hey!'" He ignored me.

Yep, some people really need to lighten up, like the bag boy I met at the grocery store the other day.

"Is plastic okay?" he asked.

"Plastic? Yes. Save a tree!" I called out, shooting a fist into the air like I'd seen activists do on television. Then I thought for a moment and added, "*However*, if the plastic is not biodegradable, it could be around forever, polluting the streams where my grandchildren and great-grandchildren will one day swim. Better make it paper."

He reached for the paper. "Okay."

"*But* if there are no trees, then photosynthesis cannot take place, and there would be no evaporation of water to form the rain clouds that make the rain that falls to fill the streams that my great-grandchildren will want to swim in. Better make it plastic."

He reached for the plastic and said, "Okay."

"*But* if we use up all the plastic now, there won't be any left for my great-grandchildren's baby bottles. Better make it paper."

He reached for the paper and said, "Okay."

"*But* if we use all the paper—never mind; I'll just carry everything in my pockets."

"Okay." And he started handing me my canned goods, green beans, pickles, applesauce . . .

I thought, *This guy has no sense of humor. As a matter of fact, he has no sense. How dense can you get? I mean—*

"Excuse me," he said, with just the faintest trace of a smile playing on his lips, just a little twitch that tugged at the corner of his mouth and threatened to take over his whole face. He took the applesauce from my hands and put it in a plastic bag. "I was just joking," he said. "Lighten up."

I took a deep breath and nodded and forced a smile. I guess good comedy can be misunderstood sometimes. Or maybe I just have to learn to lighten up.

By the way, I found that quote, and it wasn't in a medical journal after all. "A cheerful heart is good medicine, but a crushed spirit dries up the bones" (Proverbs 17:22).

Anyway, that's how things look from up here.

And Finally . . .

I've had fun with Beanie Babies, Martha Stewart, and lots of other things that get on my nerves or under my skin. So much fun I'm even planning volume two—one book just isn't enough for all the stuff I love to get up on my soapbox about. In case you hadn't noticed, sometimes I get up on my soapbox, and I can't seem to get down.

But what I want you to understand is that nothing is so trivial, nothing so mundane, that God doesn't want to be bothered with it. It's not so much *what* you bring to God, but that you bring *something*. Get up on your own soapbox and lather up about Baby Sean's refusal to take his nap or Sister Becky's commentary on your new outfit—the one you loved till she told you orange and purple don't go together. Because no matter what you bring to God, you ultimately bring yourself.

After all, you are who he wants to hear from. You are the one he cares about. "Cast all your anxiety on him," the Bible says, "because he cares for you" (1 Peter 5:7).

If God is concerned with every thought, every step, every breath we take, why do we have such a hard time sharing those details with him? "But even the petty stuff?" you say. Hey, I have petty stuff, too; that's how I filled this book! Like traffic at a standstill. Or when Zachary started to drink from a big-boy cup and started to leave big-boy stains on the living room rug. This is petty stuff, and I know it, but God cares.

So what do we say to God at times like that? We bless him, that's what. We remember his majesty, his grace, his mercy, and his love—all extended unstintingly toward us. During a price check? That's right. Bless him and build him up. Do you feel ready to pop? Do you feel the wheels coming off? Use all of those times to bless God.

Blessing God, like prayer, builds into something mighty. Things begin to change, usually starting with your face. The frowns and the scowls are replaced by smiles (yours and the little woman's who is trying to buy the house shoes with no price tag).

Our relationship with God should be grand, but we get there—as with any relationship—little by little. As we reveal ourselves to him, he reveals himself to us. Little by little, each cry, each touch, each groan to God is a small brick in a foundation that holds each of us up. If our contact with him is great and often, our foundation will be broad and solid.

Therefore, when our burdens become great, our God will sustain us. I couldn't say, "Not my will, but yours," on the big issues if I hadn't constantly been casting my cares upon him— and that means all my cares, even the petty ones.

So climb up on your soapbox and tell God how things look from up there. Let rip with what gets under your skin, gets your goat, and gets you lathered up. Go ahead. God's listening.

Anyway, that's how things look from up here.

CHONDA PIERCE INFORMATION

For other Products (videos, CDs, cassettes, etc.) by Chonda Pierce call 800-953-7878.

For Adult Preacher's Kids International information contact:

Second Row, Inc.
P.O. Box 9066
Murfreesboro, TN 37133-9066
615-848-5000
Fax: 615-848-0407
E-Mail: The2ndRow@aol.com
Website: www.chonda.org

For concert availabilities and management:

Michael Smith & Associates
1110 Brentwood Pointe
Brentwood, TN 37027
615-377-3647
Fax: 615-376-2169
E-Mail: MSmithOrg@aol.com

Life Might Be No Joke Right Now —
But Laughter Is On the Way!

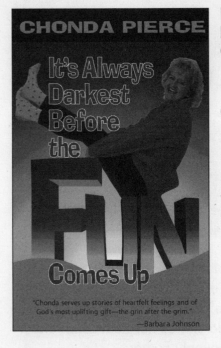

It's Always Darkest Before the Fun Comes Up

Chonda Pierce

There are two kinds of laughter. One is a hollow hilarity that masks pain too deep for words. The other is a full, joyous laugh that sounds triumphantly on the far side of life's dark passages.

Comedian Chonda Pierce knows about both kinds. In *It's Always Darkest Before the Fun Comes Up*, this spunky preacher's daughter will do more than tickle your ribs. She'll touch the place in you where laughter and tears dwell side by side. She'll show you the deep wisdom of a merry heart. And with humor and honesty, she'll reveal the God who knows how to turn life's worst punches into its most glorious punch lines — in his perfect time.

Softcover 0-310-22567-1
Audio pages 0-310-22553-1

■ ZondervanPublishingHouse
Grand Rapids, Michigan 49530
http://www.zondervan.com

Yes . . . and Amen
CD

Music has always played a vital part in Chonda's live performance and now she invites you to experience her first full-length vocal project, *Yes . . . and Amen*. Chonda had the opportunity to work with producer Mark Bright (Diamond Rio, Trisha Yearwood, and Peter Cetera) on songs that were seemingly created just for her. From the up-tempo "Whenever I Think of You" to the moving anthem "God Loves You," Chonda shares her heart and relationship with a loving Heavenly Father.

MYRRHRECORDS

Chonda Pierce On Her Soapbox
Video

Chonda Pierce has shared her unique brand of humor with over 1,000,000 people this past year. In the course of an hour she has audiences laughing, crying, and closer to understanding the grace God extends to us in the midst of trial.

Through her tongue-in-cheek delivery, Chonda lovingly pokes fun at life's daily challenges as only she can. From daily conversations between a husband and wife to Charlie's Angels . . . yes Charlie's Angels, Chonda explores different life experiences and how they mold us as people.

See Chonda on Tour—Fall 1999!

For more information on Chonda visit: www.chondapierce.com

We want to hear from you. Please send your comments about this
book to us in care of the address below. Thank you.

ZondervanPublishingHouse
Grand Rapids, Michigan 49530
http://www.zondervan.com